Reaching God Through Your PRAYERS

Vol I

Gods Unfailing Commitment

Michelle Brown

General Information

Reaching God Through Your PRAYERS
Gods Unfailing Commitment
Vol I

Cover Design: ***B.O.S.S. Publishing***

Publisher: ***Michelle Brown***

Editor: ***Terry L. Ware Sr.***

ISBN- ***978-0-578-89636-6***

1. *Spirituality* 2. *Self Help* 3. *Inspiration*

First Edition

Dedication

To my Family and Friends. To Mr. Cantey who has always been in my corner. To my team of prayer warriors who cover me. To the Victorious Praise Church family and my Pastor, Wil Nichols, for all the support, love, and teachings over the years.

Table of Contents

Reaching God Through Your PRAYERS

Vol I

Gods Unfailing Commitment

Michelle Brown

Introduction

Greetings to all and thank you for purchasing this book, I labored many years on this book. It's my desire to draw those who don't know God, those on the verge of hopelessness, new believers, those who want to experience God more intimately, even those on the fence with Christianity and Religion. Why? Because they have the most need. Who will share what God has done for them and help them to develop their God given purpose? We are called to do it. God has equipped His people, whom He called, to reach those who need Him. Then, this book is to those who know Christ, have a relationship with God, have given their life to God, and want to develop a better prayer life.

Prayer:

I pray for all those reading and who will read this book. Open their minds, hearts, and ears to hear what You speak to them and particularly while they're reading this book. May this book reach those who may seem unreachable. God, I pray for a supernatural experience for everyone, I pray that their lives be changed, and renewed. I pray for better understanding. I pray this book will bless their lives and draw people to You God. I pray this book renews and cause us to return to You with greater passion, greater strength, greater power. God, I pray You get us back on our knees, back seeking You in prayer for everything and reaching out to You in prayer for the answers and solutions. In Jesus Name, we declare it is so, Amen.

~Michelle~

Chapter 1

Keys to Reaching

Gods Ear

God gives us lots of instructions. It's like if we go to work out and they say you must stretch first, then follow this plan to lose the weight or get healthy. And if we follow the instructions, it will give us change, results that we want, maybe to lose 20 pounds, or to lose inches, or maybe to tone a certain area like abs or arms. We will get the ultimate results because we followed the instructions. And that's very much like God's plan. He lays out a blueprint, a map, a meal plan, step by step instructions and the results that we will reap from it IF we abide.

Malachi 3:10 (KJV)

Bring ye all the tithes into the storehouse, that there may be meat in mine house, and prove me now herewith, saith the LORD of hosts, if I will not open you the windows of heaven, and pour you out a blessing, that there shall not be room enough to receive it.

He gives instruction, commands, and then He tells us why He wants us to do that. Lastly It tells us what we will reap from it.

***Key 1: We must do what He ask of* us**

God makes a promise. If we do these 4 things, I will do this. But the key to God doing His part is we have to also do our part. We want His blessings without the alignment or changing our ways and that's impossible. Alignment is necessary. Let's break this down for understanding.

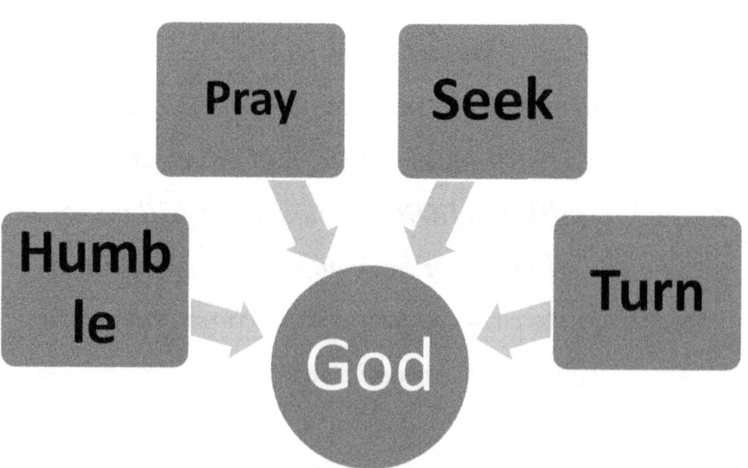

Reaching God Through Your Prayers

2 Chronicles 7: 14 (KJV)

If my people, which are called by my name, shall humble themselves, and pray, and seek my face, and turn from their wicked ways; THEN will I hear from heaven, and will forgive their sin, and will heal their land.

Humbleness (Meekness)- not thinking to highly of oneself. **Pray**- communicate with God regardless, if it's for yourself or others. **Seek**- running after Him with all your strength and might, learning more of Him daily or all that your able, search to grow more like Him and to know more of His word, and **Turn**- from those things that cause you to stumble in your walk, places, people, thoughts etc.

Let me share a little more things that make you want to call your ex or music that makes you wanna have sex. (These are just examples☺) Because let's be honest some music will put you in the mood of temptation. Temptation starts in your mind then goes to your actions. It puts your feelings in the mood to do things you otherwise would not have done. So, for this reason doing what you must do (deleting numbers, blocking text, contacts, emails, etc.) to keep your mind from going to the next stage may keep from wrongdoing. Just like when we listen to worship music, for me it ushers in the presence of God, so the opposite is true for what some of us call worldly music. There is certain music I don't listen to because I want to continue in my thoughts of holiness and being pure before the Lord. This scripture has helped me in my ability to live right. All parts of this scripture are so necessary but that *turning away* stuck like glue, because not turning away keeps us from being obedient. We cannot be obedient without turning away from sin and things that take us out of alignment. God says after the conditions have been met, that I require of you, **then (Then: after that, next, afterward) I will hear from heaven, forgive their sins, and will heal their land.**

God promises to do this:

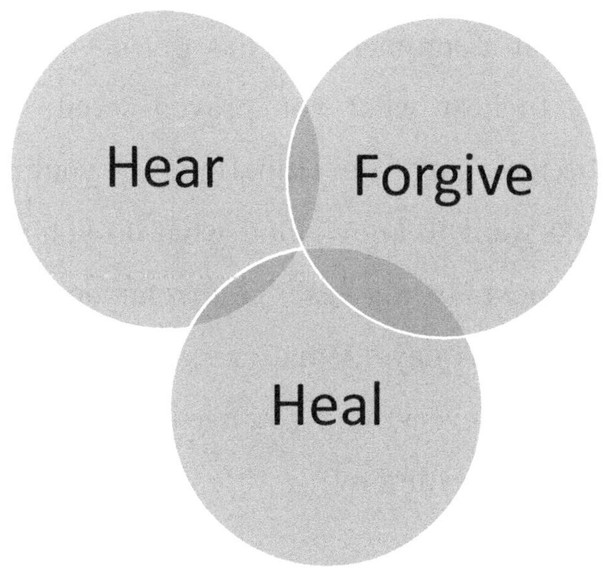

<u>Hear</u>

Sometimes there are situations that can cloud your ability to hear God. Sin, Stress, Busy Schedules are a few. Sometimes we can be so busy that we don't even have time for God or the things of God. This places things before God: hectic work schedule, rushing to get there and rushing back, family and the household demands, what I call lollygagging, which is doing nothing, but still wasting time like watching hours of television, even a lot of church work can pull you away from the personal assignment He has given you. God promises to hear what you prayed about, what you've been seeking from Him. It may be your next move, you want to know, God what do you want me to do next. In my case: God reminded me, I heard it clear as day. "What are you waiting for, I've given you everything you need." (See chapter 3 for complete testimony)

Forgive

I know sometimes we feel like it's impossible that someone can love us that much that they will forgive all we have done that was contrary. The word says He will cast all our sins into the depths of the sea. Micah 7:19, someone else said it like this: He will throw your sins in the sea of forgetfulness.

That is far, far away. In the deep water, in a place that it's hard to get to. It's like when somebody commits a homicide and takes the body and ties it to a brick and drops it to the bottom of the sea. Ok, I watch too many crime shows. Let me continue. God loves us this much because He wants you to succeed. He wants you to be whole. He wants to get the glory from your life, He want His plan fulfilled. He wants to forgive you so you can go ahead and live your best life without guilt, shame, condemnation, or fear. Receive it today.

Heal

Then we must allow God to work through us. For example, like a mechanic, they take the old parts or parts that don't work properly, that may be broken, that are worn so the car may jerk or cut off, and they replace them, so it runs smoothly. Take out the stony heart and fill it with a loving heart. Take a cold and callus heart and replace it with a caring heart. God needs to heal us because a broken and hurting person cannot complete the task God has set, it would be too difficult to stay on task. God must heal us of relationships and hurts. God must heal us from past hurts of family and friends and God must heal us from betrayal and hurts from those we trusted, coworkers, business partners etc. We can't heal until we heal. There are certain people God need you to bless but, we must allow God to heal and search through us so we can do the healing He wants to do through us for others. I learned over the years to go to God about me. Not always going to God about others. But asking God, did I say it wrong? Was my attitude off? was I loving? Was there anything I could have done better to bring you glory? Of course, getting to this place won't be easy, it wasn't for me, and it won't be for you. It was years that I decided I don't want a half relationship; I don't want people broken from something I said or done. Get this, EVEN IF THEY WERE THE ONES WHO WRONGED ME. THAT WAS MY BIGGEST PROBLEM. I

WANTED TO GET BACK AT THOSE WHO HURT ME. It took years! It may take time, but it's so worth it.

Key 2: Gods divine plan for our life

"There is a time and season for everything." Ecclesiastes 3: 1, to everything there is a season, and a time to every purpose under the heavens. Not ***some things***, not what we think is important, ALL THINGS. So sometimes we pray for things, and they may be in His will, however it will happen on God's time not our timetable on when we want it to happen. Some of us make our plan of what we want to do, "we want to finish this by the next 2 years, do this in the next year", etc., for our lives and expect God to bless it. How did you even get to that plan, did it come from laying before the Lord, was it a burning desire in your heart, was it a gift or hobby you had. It's ok to make plans but we need to ask God "IS THIS ALIGNED WITH THE PLAN AND WILL YOU HAVE FOR MY LIFE?

We need to ask God to SHAPE AND MOLD THE PLAN THAT WE HAVE, WITH HIS PLAN"!

Jeremiah 29:11 says, I know the thoughts that I think towards you sayeth the Lord, thoughts of peace and not evil to bring you to an EXPECTED END. NIV says, I know the plans that I have for you, plans to prosper you, and not harm you, and plans to give you hope and a future. He expects us to do what He has planned, and furthermore we should delight in doing His Will. GODS EXPECTED PLAN & GODS EXPECTED END.

Jeremiah 1:5 (KJV)

Before I formed thee in the belly, I knew thee; and before thou camest forth out of the womb I sanctified thee, and I ordained thee a prophet unto the nations.

Key 3: We must ask Him

This is the confidence that we have in Him, that if we ask anything according to His will, He hears us. 1 John 5:14, "IF WE ASK"- the first hurdle we must get over is just the fact of having enough faith to *ask*, even if it's a small amount of faith like the bible says, the size of a mustard seed. Matthew 17:20, but our lack of faith keeps us from talking to God. I believe shame keeps us from God too, sometimes we don't believe He will work it out, we don't believe He hears us, we don't believe that we are even worthy to go to Him or receive from Him. All of these are some reasons that keep us from communication with God: SIMPLY ASKING! Jesus calls the disciples faithless in Matthew 17:17 because they didn't have enough faith to believe they could cast out the devil in the child with seizures even though the power was given to do so, Luke 10:19.

Going to God and asking Him for various things in our life also takes confidence. Yes, we need confidence in ourselves to achieve the things we want in life, to put into action the goals etc. But the confidence in going to God in prayer is being confident in Him, not your own ability but in God's power through our prayer to fix and handle anything you brought before Him. So many of us go to everybody else but God, we ask family what we should do, we go to our friends to get their opinions, yes even our spiritual counsel first. But the first person we need to go to is God. We must do our part and go before the Lord, nothing is off limits, ask Him about whatever it is you're seeking. Take it all to Him, what we do is pick and choose what we decide to let God handle and which ones we want to handle. We must relinquish and give it all to Him, all the situations, all the issues, the sin, all the struggles, take it all to Him in prayer. LEAVE IT IN HIS HANDS TO WORK IT OUT FOR YOU. LEAVE IT IN HIS HANDS TO SHOW YOU THE NEXT MOVE TO MAKE, WITH THE THINGS YOU'VE PRAYED TO HIM ABOUT.

Key 4: It's according to "His Will"

The second hurdle given in 1 John 5; the latter part of this verse talks about asking but specifically regarding His will for our lives. We must align our prayers, our asking to His plan; God let Your will be done in this situation. God let Your will be done in my life, Ask Him according to His will. Lord is this the will You have for me, the way You would have for me to go. Ask God to reveal what His will is for you. God show me Your will. We must also make sure our motives and the things we are asking for are not worldly.

I went to God about my finances, and I told God I want to give more, bless me so that I can do that, and He did. God wants His church to grow, and He wants you to grow, and we need resources for that. So, God did what I desired of Him to do, be it so because its Gods will that the house of God and your house is provided for. We must ask for things that will help us be better Christians, better parents, help us serve better, do ministry successfully, family and marriages, all things that God are concerned with, should be our concern and our prayers. James 4 lets us know that we have not because we ask not and when we do ask, we are asking for the wrong things.

Key 5: Living Right

1 Peter 3:12, for the eyes of the Lord are on the righteous and His ears are open to their prayers. Let me ask a question, could our lifestyle decisions be causing God not to bless us as He planned in His will? For the scripture doesn't say the Lords eyes are on us all, it says HIS EYES ARE ON THE RIGHTEOUS, His ears are on their prayers, again it doesn't say all. This lets us know that the way we live does play apart. A lot of us want to live the way we want to live, though it may be opposite of what God said. These scriptures speak Holy living= open ears/eyes with you. That school you want to complete and didn't know how it would get done, He will see to it that it's done for those, the Righteous. Desires to do big things, get a house, a husband, new car, business resources, that child you and your spouse desire. I'M a witness, GOD BLESSES THE RIGHTEOUS.

THE WILLING AND **OBEDIENT**, THERE IT IS AGAIN. SHALL EAT THE FRUIT OF THE LAND. Isiah 1:19. Those who do right when no one's looking, you apologize for things you know you did no wrong (bless are the peace makers for they shall inherit the land), you treat your enemies, frenemies with love, those who do what the word says, use the word as their compass, not what the world says you should do but go and seek what God said you should do. Those kinds.

Have you ever heard the saying that we derailed? I think sometimes we do go down alleys and valleys and turns, roads and detours that God did not intend us to take. Yes, we can get back on track of doing and living the way He has asked. But it will be a choice that needs to be made daily to live a Holy consecrated life. Because we know that His will for our lives is perfect. Obedience to Gods will and God's word is key. The willing and obedient you will eat the fruit of the land. There are two commands in that scripture ***be willing and***

be obedient. Placing emphasis on our living right is important to our blessings and as 1Peter shares, it keeps Gods ears open to us. This scripture has also helped me to live right. Reminding me my obedience plays a part in my success or failure.

Key 6: Your experiences with God matters

Most of us have had quite a few experiences with God and if we've been saved for a while, most of us have had a lot of experiences. We have a track record with Him just like He has with us. God has seen all we've said and all we've done. He sees all our giving, He sees our faith etc. Our track record, with a lot of us, He has done things in our lives that we know it was only Him; job positions, financial blessings, and kept us from dangers that had the danger came upon us, we would've deserved, but thank God, He didn't allow it. For me the list is long. There were car accidents, bad decisions, suicide attempts. I once said, I wonder what it feels like to run this car into the ocean. But I have also had countless of ways made, 30-60 and YES, 100-

fold blessings. Positions I didn't qualify for, and favor from God that I know was only Him, etc.

Our prayers to God based on experience gives us boldness. You did it before and I know You can do it again. More standing power because we know He is a God that answers, HE'S DONE IT BEFORE! It gives us a boost of faith because we have these mental points in our head of all He has done in the past, and it also keeps us while we're going through our present circumstances. Some of us the devil is attacking on every side. Like the word says, TROUBLED ON EVERY SIDE. But God can keep you, deliver you, strengthen you etc., based solely on what He has already done for you. We also know He already promises to bless our future as well, ***everything that your hands shall touch SHALL be blessed, Deuteronomy 28. Everywhere that your feet shall tread shall be yours, Joshua 1:3.***

Think back to all the trying times you have had in your life, your past experiences. Some of us our prayers change when we get in sticky situations and then we go back to not talking to God when things get good again. If you think back, you will see His hands that protected, that provided, that kept you in your right mind even though you were very sure you would lose it. All those experiences have given God a 100% track record to be trusted in the future. Not only to be trusted but to take all the situations to Him in prayer to work out. There has been so much I just can't tell it all. I know people say that as a cliché, but it really is true in every area of my life He has shown Himself to be a constant thing that never changes and keeps His promises. I am God I change not, Malachi 3.

I remember when I was in school driving 20 minutes each way and my car broke down in my last semester, I didn't know how I would get to school and if I would finish, He made a way. Who can you think of that has never went back on their word, hasn't failed to deliver the promise they made? I just had a client break a promise last week. It happens. By nature, we are flawed and fail each other. The bible says our righteousness is like filthy rags, Isaiah 64. Only with God can we learn to take on His characteristics and become more like Him. Dying daily to self. Some of us must die minute by minute, hour by hour, praying to God, Lord hold my tongue, Lord zip my mouth. I've been there and if that's what's required to stay saved and sanctified, do so. It does get easier because you begin to master what tried to master you. Over time you start to feel and see the signs and calm your storms within. Still thinking about your experiences: Let me ask, WHEN HAS GOD EVER FAILED?

Let's go a step further. Some may say I can't think of anything God has done for me. If you can't think of anything He has done for you, then you can look on the experiences of others (God has no respect of persons), their current and past experiences, a friend, a family member. To be honest yes, we all are at different levels, different gifts, (etc.), within our relationship with God and the word says the closer we draw to Him the closer He will draw to us, James 4. Actually, though you may feel God is not there or has done nothing HE HAS. We have natural blessings, if you are breathing, you didn't pay him for that air. You get 24hrs a day, if you are reading this book that lets me know your eyes work, He opens most of our eyes daily whether we are worthy or not. Air and water we need, He freely gives us. These are constant natural blessings we receive daily. So, based on just that, we all have so much He has done whether naturally or spiritually. But some of us have also had a lot of spiritual experiences, I've noticed God's abundance of spiritual blessings; dreams, visions, signs, healings, anointing on my prayers, Holy Spirit encounters (etc.) not only when I was going to church regularly, studying like I should and praying constantly, but even more when I gave up on church, thank You God. I remember telling God I was never going back to church. It was many years back I said, God if this is what church is about, if this is what church people are like, I don't want it and vowed to never go back again. In all honesty during this wilderness experience I felt the Holy Spirit like I never have in all my years as a Christian and all my years on the earth. Thank You, Father. God was with me in the good times with my walk with Him and Thanks be unto God, He had to dry many, many tears, many broken hearts, when I was talked about, when I was betrayed, when friends left and no one to call, He never left. He was there to carry me when I was weak and pick me up when I was down. He's there in the ups and downs of our experiences. In the highs of my experiences with Him, I was so hungry for the word. I would study for hours a day. I remember I would go to the library or coffee shop and stay there for hours and hours studying and going without food, and I didn't even want to get up to go to the bathroom, because it was so satisfying, so fulfilling I didn't even get hungry. He sustained my business traveling to all the major cities and my household, all sustained. My hunger for His word was stronger than anything else, I would have 4 and 5 books and bibles in front of me, it consumed me, this was the case even when it came to work. When you're self-employed if you don't work and get things done, THERES NO CHECK COMING AT THE END OF THE WEEK!

I remember praying to God to make ways so I could study and read the word like I knew I needed to for where He was taking me. HE ALWAYS DID! I will also say that this was the start of when I noticed a very strong Holy Spirit indwelling. Some may say its spooky, I remember the outer body experiences I had, I now know that was the Holy Spirit letting me know, I'm here, I got you, I'm your helper and boy oh boy did He teach me and do some wondrous things in my life, EXPERIENCES. This is also the time He brought up my calling to preach again though I thought I had gotten away from it, every excuse I could think of; God you got the wrong one was my #1 saying, I defeated myself, I didn't believe in myself, I discredited my own self. I didn't need others to do it for me back then, saying I don't have a perfect life, I'm not qualified, I don't think I can do this. What will people think? Will they accept me? On and on, but in my experience, God called me after some major blows in my life and kept confirming it during trials and bumps in my life.

Let me go a little deeper on this. That's why the word says test and trials come to make us strong. He spoke the most in the trials. Now, we know God makes no mistakes. He kept telling me even though I told myself I'm not the one. HE KEPT ON SAYING, YOU! I say all this to say, God is not just interested in your life when you feel like you are being a good Christian or let's keep it real or if you are being Christ like at all. Even when less than perfect, if you pay attention, He's there then as well. Romans 5, While we were yet sinners Christ died.

You can base your prayers and your faith on the testimonies He has given yourself and others. For me there has been many. *They overcame him (devil) by the blood of the lamb and by the words of their testimonies, Rev 12:11.* Reminding God, You did it before. You blessed me before, look how You kept me the last time; I thought this was the end of me and I'm still here. God, I've seen You heal others; I know You can do the same for me. God, I seen You spare lives, God do it for me. Praying to God based on experiences speaks of your faith in God to work in your future experiences.

Key 7: It must be in the "RIGHT NAME"

Peter said, don't think it was by our power, our strength, our holiness. Let me paraphrase; don't think we did this on our own; don't think it was because of me. BUT ONLY ONE NAME. The name that's above every name, IN THE NAME OF JESUS CHRIST. See also Acts 3:11-16

Acts 4:10 (KJV)

Be it known unto you all, and to all the people of Israel, that by the name of Jesus Christ of Nazareth, whom ye crucified, whom God raised from the dead, even by him doth this man stands here before you whole.

Peter wanted to set the record straight so that no one could credit him, glory his name or magnify or give him honor. Lift God and He will lift you up.

There is our power when we call on the Name of Jesus. Just as Peter prayed and had faith to believe that his healing came through that name, we must have that same faith and believe that that same power, that in prayer we can cast down devils, we can raise up weak bodies and minds that are lost. We also have power to heal, set free, and deliver ourselves and others. The Bible says greater works we shall do, John 14:12. Whatever we need, whatever we need deliverance from, whatever the situation, we must pray from a sincere heart lifting our request to God in the name of Jesus our Savior. That makes all the difference.

Notes:

Chapter 2

The Importance of Prayer

The bible tells us to pray without ceasing. So that tells me we are to pray as often as we can. There is no set time or place to pray. I believe we need to turn off the TVs and social media ***intentionally*** to spend time with God and to *commune with Him in prayer,* it is so necessary. Also avoiding silly talks and games that we can call timewasters or irrelevant conversations, which the bible says such talk led to more ungodliness, 1 Timothy 4:7. When we replace those things with prayer and study we will see changes in our life, the way we think, how powerful our prayer life will grow. Confidence when praying, more power in prayers because of being filled with His word, He will just bring it out as you pray, He will give you what to say. He pulls at your heart and drops bits and pieces in your spirit that will be what people, even yourself, will need. He brings it back up to you when you get in a bind or get down. God may say daughter/son, I got you, and I'll never leave you. Daughter: give it to Me vengeance is mine, Son:

My grace is sufficient; He can remind and encourage you because it's planted down inside of you already. The word even says the Holy Spirit intercedes for us.

Romans 8:26 (KJV), Likewise the Spirit also helpeth our infirmities: for we know not what we should pray for as we ought: but the Spirit itself maketh intercession for us with groanings which cannot be uttered. If the word is not in your heart, mind, and in your spirit for Him to bring back to your remembrance then sometimes we may feel like we have nothing to say, we feel all hope is gone and nowhere to turn. These are the times that we crash, we give up, we get upset, we lose it and do things we OTHERWISE would not have done. We are weak and need to be rebuilt, recharged, get refueled, feed your spirit. We can always pray and tell Him how we feel, share our innermost thoughts. It's the safest place to talk. There is no one better to talk to. Tell Him what you're thankful for, thank Him for providing, thank Him for protection, but also doubts, fears, questions, concerns etc. Not only will we see change in our personal life but collectively we will also see changes in our families, schools, churches, and communities.

Another importance to prayer, is ***timing***. Going to God or going before the Lord in prayer where we don't have to worry about interruptions, where we can talk to Him in peace. If you want to sit and chat with Him for hours at a time, we so need it, you can. Where the Spirit can speak to you and it's a quiet still voice, 1 King 19:12. This is one reason why I like a quiet house at any time of the day. But for me early in the morning (I call it the prayer warrior hours: before 7am) before every one wakes up, before the day gets started of work, kids, school and all our other daily task, (Jesus went away to an uninterrupted place early morning before daybreak, Mark 1:35) or late at night when all the chores are done everyone is in bed and you can have your one-on-one time, that I think is a must. It is so necessary. Because otherwise we just drift from day to day and not feeding our souls and minds with what God said would keep us. He promises us that it would be our strength, it would guide, and protect, and keep our minds. I will keep the in perfect peace whose mind is stayed on me, Isiah 26:3.

Could this be the reason why so many people are losing it? I can only speak about me, there are times when I allowed my mind or gave it permission, (not casting it down) to say things and it took me out of my peace. Be honest, what about you? ***The absence of your peace is the beginning and leads to worry, stress, fear, anxiety, depression, and spills into your physical realm as pains, heart attacks, overeating, and other health issues***. All because one choice of putting our mind on other things when God has promised if we keep Him, His word, meditating on it day and night that it would keep us. That is our prescription. So, when we don't take His medicine we wonder why we're still sick. Is it safe to say we are basically showing God, *I DON'T BELIEVE WHAT YOU SAID, I DON'T BELIEVE THAT IT WILL KEEP ME*! Some have taken medicine that altered brain cells and changed the way one thinks when God gave us the answers on what to think on. Mediate on the word and if you must, just like the word says day and night, Psalms 1:2. Think good things also. Whatever is pure and just if there be any good report think on these things, Philippians 4:8. Some do have imbalances and need medication, still praying for complete healing. We must renew our minds and pray to God to help and intervene. So, I said that to say, it's so important that we take ***limitations off our prayer life***, which is what I want to share next. We want God's voice and Gods hands to flow, so I've found removing limitations off Him is so necessary. If He wakes you up early in the morning and you can't go back to sleep, pray; if He wakes you up in the middle of the night, pray. If you're lying-in bed and can't sleep, pray. Oh man have I had some great times with God when He wakes me up like that. Yes, I said He woke me up, because He knows what we need and He will do what He needs to, to get our attention, no matter the timing. We need time with Him! And *He knows what He needs to say to you,* for you and others. *Remember He knows our plan.* It's up to us to align ourselves enough to hear Him, quiet our lives enough to hear Him and walk closer with Him for His guidance. If you stand at a football field one person at one end and you at the other and they scream something at you. You will not hear clearly it may sound like a squirrel munching. But the closer you bring yourself in to the other person, it gets clearer and clearer the closer you come in. Thank you, Father, it's the same way with God. If you've never heard God whisper to you or warn you or encourage you. I would say spend some quiet time with Him. Many times, if I'm talking on and on, He will say be quiet. Times I wanted to react quickly to a text or a call, in defense and He will say no or immediately give me a scripture to remind me this is how I want you to do this, this is how I want you to act and say and represent me on the earth. God woke me up many times and now I try to keep a notepad and pen to write down what He says, shows, or does.

I have been awakened to visions and dreams that scared me, I was asking the Lord was this for me, was it to share with someone, some dreams of family and others. I asked should I share this or should I not because they were so detailed and graphic. Sometimes I went to others I trusted about things God had shown me, that may add to what I was experiencing and could shed some light. In some cases, this has happened, and the person would say yes God deals with me like that too. Placing limits on prayer time or study time could be a hindrance to you when He wants to speak or when He may be leading you to a specific scripture to study or something that He really needs to share with you to get His work completed. If you called someone and every time you call, they say I'll call you back only when it was convenient for them or not call back at all, how would you feel? In this same way, we must treat our prayer time as of high importance.

I've had so many of these experiences where one specific scripture will stay on my mind or keep popping up and then I'll study it and it was the missing point for a sermon, a few times He has led me to do studies and I'd get to church to discover it was the main scripture of the preachers' message. I find it so warming when God does this, some have never had these experiences and I think as people of God we must share, so that others will have a hunger to experience Him like this. Being close with God is so fulfilling, He said draw nigh to me (close) and I'll draw nigh to you, James 4:8. If you desire to be closer, hear from him more, feel his presence more, do more for God. Study more, pray more, serve more, lay before Him in expectation to hear from Him and you will experience the presence of the Holy Spirit. ***BUT THE MOST IMPORTANT ONE: LIVE RIGHT! DO RIGHT!***

Why limit praying to God to when you awake in the morning or at night, when we can continually pray to Him *ANYTIME*; in a business meeting or sitting in class, pray throughout the day. The Bible tells us that men ought to always pray and not faint, Luke 18:1. Praying constantly helps me to stay spiritual or as some may say "Helps me to stay save" with a focus mind on the things of the (God) Spirit. Walk in the Spirit and you *shall not* fulfill the lust of your flesh, Galatians 5:16. That "***shall not***" pops out so loud to me, He didn't say maybe, but it ***shall not***! This is important to us as believers, having the ability to stand on the word, the promises of God, when your flesh tells you to SNAP! Thank you, Jesus! Take a trip with me, you been walking in the spirit all day and praying, Do you see it: that calm you, the car that cut you off didn't bother you, what people say comes in one ear and rolls out fast in the other, you're slower to say things to people who offend you, or you actually say the words God gave to you to say this time, because you're so in tune with the Spirit. Oh, what a great trip! Praying in advance or immediately as situations arises helps us avoid things that could cause us to get upset, angry or just making costly decisions we would not have made had we been walking with God. I can say with confidence this time can save marriages, family squabbles, work tension and many misunderstandings. Also, what is important is a prayer partner.

Acts 4:24, and when they heard that, *they lifted up their voice to God* with one accord, and said, Lord, thou art God, which hast made heaven, and earth, and the sea, and all that in them is (see also Acts 4:31). These scriptures speak to the power of unity, power of relationships, and the power that we have when we connect by going to God for ourselves and others. Pray that God send people that you can pray with, someone you can trust and be willing to be open about any struggles or questions/concerns, people that are spiritually mature, and in turn pray that God send you to people who need the same, Divine Connections, these connections are so needed. I have several and it definitely helps when you have been before the Lord, and it seems that He's not answering. 1 can chase 1,000, 2 can put 10,000 to flight, Deuteronomy 32:30. We can be stronger together in prayer and in life in general. We lift each other spirits, we keep each other accountable, we love on each other without conditions, and we celebrate each other just because we want the other person to be happy and full of joy, we want our friends and family to have spiritual maturity. Called people want to see people who are hurting, FREE. We lean on each other in times of difficulties, pray for each other even before they ask or even if they never ask. We pray with each other standing together for whatever petitions our sisters or brothers are taking to God. Basically, being a witness that we know when we pray God hears us, when we pray, He will answer, and that there is unity and strength in praying together. Where 2 or 3 gather in my name, there I will be in the mist, Matthew 18:20. We also need to pray for wisdom and understanding for however He chooses to answer, and it may not be to our liking.

I'm a witness to this, a lot of times God will drop people in your spirit and ***ITS FOR A REASON***. To pray for them or maybe they have a need, or you have some sort of resource that could benefit them, vice versa. I have gotten better about reaching out to those people when this happens. Each time God has done this the person was in great need. The bible says we don't always know what we should pray for, but the spirit will intercede for us, Romans 8:26, and I do just that, in these times I don't have a pre-created list of what I'm going to say to a person, as you communicate with them God will give you what to say and what to do, what to pray about. Sometimes while you are with them, He will drop hints on what you may need to share with them. Maybe a testimony or maybe what you need to pray for on their behalf. You may hold their hands and cry with them praying silently or just a hug and pray to oneself. You may say nothing, just sit to keep them company. I think it's also important to be you, be natural. We need each other; we so desperately need the support of each other regardless of what some may think, feel, or what the devil may plant in your mind, "I don't need nobody". It's a lie. The devil can really work in the minds and hearts of those who have no friends, loners, people who feel like no one cares, GIVE SPECIAL ATTENTION TO THOSE KIND IN MY OPINION, those who block themselves from church people because some say we can be so fake and those who feel like they have no one they can count on. I challenge you to seek people like such since God has no respect of persons, we want all Gods people to be loved and accepted and grow to their full potential that God has for them, and we can help in that. Luke 22:31, And the Lord said, Simon, Simon, behold, satan hath desired to have you, that he may sift you as wheat; 32: But I have prayed for thee, that thy faith fails not: and when thou art converted, strengthen thy brethren.

God knows how important prayer and being there for one another is. We are called to strengthen each other. We need to cover each other, protect each other, to repent and forgive. I loved visiting my grandma, she said to me during one of our talks, "forgive and do it quickly". When people come and confide in you, trusting you with valuable information, be found trustworthy. Finally, encourage each other to greatness; greatness in the area of their spiritual life, prayer, and other things too. Pray for them and help, ye which are spiritual restore in meekness, Galatians 6:1. Those who love the Lord are about Kingdom building, seeing others winning and blessed even when it's not them. Sharing knowledge to help restore someone. ***THIS IS PRICELESS.***

Notes:

Chapter 3

Personal Experiences

- *Prayers, -Visions, -Dreams -Prophecy*

Lots of experiences are included here as well as things God has done. What has been shared, I believe they will bless your life and may look familiar to you, as God has given us so many encounters with Him to grasp our attention. I launched a prayer ministry after I saw God anoint my prayers. I remember being timid and what I think of as an unfruitful prayer life before, to bold spirit filled prayers with confidence as He increased my gifts, gifts that at this time I had never asked for. After I matured and was being developed, much study and experiences, I started asking God specifically about increasing my gifts, anoint me, to fill me with various gifts. The word says we should desire the best gifts.

1Corithians 14:1 (NIV)
Follow the way of love and eagerly desire gifts of the Spirit, especially prophecy.

1Corithians 14:1 (KJV)

Follow after charity, and desire spiritual gifts, but rather that ye may prophesy.

I still do this, as I matured in my walk, I started asking God for gifts, one I asked for was prophecy and He fulfilled. Although when He started showing me things, I got a little defensive, saying things like "God why would You show me this and not fully show me who this is for? Are you trying to warn me? Is this something I need to share? Is it for someone else?" I didn't understand Gods gifting in my life.

Singing as a little girl, they use to stick me and my cousin on the front row. When I served at the shelter the ladies asked, "will you sing for me?" God anointed my prayers, and I noticed the difference when I open my mouth, I knew it was God because sometimes I couldn't even remember what was said but someone would contact me and say your prayer blessed me. Also, a gift I was blessed with, I didn't ask for: speaking in tongues, crying out to the Lord and He filled my mouth. I do remember it was while I was in the presence of the Holy Spirit. At home and church. Oh, how amazed I am that God bestows upon us and trusts us with these gifts. His gifts and callings are without repentance, Romans 11:29. Although I must be honest and share, I believe sin separates us from God. What I mean by separation is when we don't study or pray or give Him the time required, it clouds things. I've seen times when I was a babe in Christ and what my prayers were then, if at all, to what my prayer life is now. I prayed and gave it to God. I have seen God's power so many times, over and repeatedly. I think when we have these encounters with God it's impossible to doubt what He says and what He shows because He has shown up before, so you know what it looks and feels like. To me it's impossible to doubt what you know about Him, because you have personally experienced Him.

Ok, I'm going to take us all back to my dirt road country church days of singing in the choir, church all day, choir anniversaries, marching in, what great memories. You know the sayings you may have heard in churches where they do foot stomping, double clapping, tambourines, and baptism in a real lake and use wash boards and a stick to make melodies unto the Lord. I remember hearing my grandma singing hymns like: "REAL, Jesus is real to me, oh yes, He gave me the victory, so many people doubt Him, I know too much about Him, that is why I love Him so cause He's so real to me." The saying "you can't make me doubt Him, I know too much about Him", that's what I'm trying to say. God has done so much no matter what season,

Your experiences with Him become your faith.

Ahead you will find some of my personal experiences with God, they have been many, some have been very big, and some have been small, but I think you will agree with me that just the fact of God thinking enough to speak and send us nuggets to help us, is mind blowing. That out of all the trillions and trillions of prayers and people that love Him, He still has time to see about me and you. As you read my experiences, ask yourself what has God spoken to me? What do you want to say to God? Ask God to speak to you. What do you believe God is moving you to do? What scripture did He bring to mind?

My Experiences:

~~~~~~~~~~~~~~~~~~~~~~~~~~~~~~~~~~~

During one of my fasting times, I decided to get out the house and get some fresh air, I walked in the bookstore and was roaming around in the Christian section. I wasn't looking for anything particular, but the first book I grabbed off the shelf was called, The Fasting Bible. It was like God Himself saying, learn of me. I sat down and studied almost 10 different fasting's of the bible. (2013)

~~~~~~~~~~~~~~~~~~~~~~~~~~~~~~~~~~~

A first lady of a mega church called my business and came in for a consultation, she told me God told her to bless my business. She got a $1200 service. God knows what you need and will send help and others to bless you. (2016)

~~~~~~~~~~~~~~~~~~~~~~~~~~~~~~~~~~~

As I sat in service something came over me. Yes, its normal for a child of God to feel the presence of God. A dance, shout, but this time it was different. As I worshipped, the Preacher was on stage and had her
~~~~~~~~~~~~~~~~~~~~~~~~~~~~~~~~~~~

warrior team around her, she was holding her belly. It didn't feel like pains but a move of God taking over, a release, a leaping in my belly. The same way I was witnessing the Preacher, I found myself in the same position. Over the days I tried to understand what took place as I never experienced this before. I believe God is birthing great things in our lives, His plans are great, His power in our lives unfathomed. Get ready for what God is doing through you, God is gonna birth His plan through His earthen vessels. And God spoke to me like never before the years following. (2017)

~~~~~~~~~~~~~~~~~~~~~~~~~~~~~~~~~

God had begun to show me a lot of gifts by this time, it was very early in the morning, did I think I was worthy of all His gifts He bestowed? No! But I knew that Him giving me more gifts was not about me, but the work He wanted to do through me, this gift of prophecy was new to me, and it was very detailed. This gift came after consecrated time of giving myself to Him and it was very unexpected. At first, I asked God a lot of questions, but then I got out of my carnal mind and
~~~~~~~~~~~~~~~~~~~~~~~~~~~~~~~~~

applied what I knew about His gifts and prayed about it. I also sought understanding from holy women and men of God who helped me. God showed me a pickup truck, it was dark blue, reminded me of a F150. It was somewhat cloudy like the dusk of day early in the morning before it turns daytime, and the lights were flickering back and forth as if to get someone's attention. So, I started praying: God what is this, is this for someone and if I need to share it with them? Are You trying to warn me of something? Are You trying to get my attention with something? It's so imperative that we quiet our lives to be able to hear and recognize God, Seek Him and His word about what He reveals to us. (2018)

~~~~~~~~~~~~~~~~~~~~~~~~~~~~~~~~

During a time in my career, it seemed to me like blessings were falling left and right. I was approved by 3 State Boards to teach instructors and licensees and I didn't even have an instructor's license at the time, my instructor license came years later. I was chosen to teach at the largest trade show, Bronner Bros show opening the doors for me to embark upon speaking engagements
~~~~~~~~~~~~~~~~~~~~~~~~~~~~~~~~

and be recognized as a National Educator, I was chosen out of a pool of educators to teach in Las Vegas. I was the only African American on the panel to teach, that class sold out with 200+ people, they provided a contract and flew me in. She called me after the class because on top of what the contract had stated. She said the class was so profitable they wanted to send me another check. My business was very profitable then, writing hundreds of dollars in tithing checks weekly and my company that provided continuing education made thousands of dollars per class, with my team of 5-6 educators teaching 21 classes with me, the largest company for Continuing Education in NC. God's hand was upon me, His favor on my life, I clearly saw. He told us we would have favor with God and man, Proverbs 3:4. Thank You God!

~~~~~~~~~~~~~~~~~~~~~~~~~~~~~~~~

I was working for a company and things seemed off, and I wanted my own salon. I started praying and I prayed very specific, about a business location and I told God the street and pass what street that I wanted my business because I had already done my homework and
~~~~~~~~~~~~~~~~~~~~~~~~~~~~~~~~

researched the demographics of the area, the exact area I wanted to be in. God made it happen! Exactly what I prayed, exact street and pass the street I specifically prayed about. He blessed my business with 10+ on my team and a multicultural client base. $900 and $1100 per service. Those resources allowed me to fund and serve the homeless, among other things, we teamed with others and bought 100 Christmas gifts one year for the homeless and continued feeding, praying, and passing out bibles. After a setback, God will give you a comeback and bless you with the desires of your heart. God knew I needed resources to do what He put my hands to and He did so. (2005)

~~~~~~~~~~~~~~~~~~~~~~~~~~~~~~~~~

Walking down the street, I lived close to work, so I decided to walk home and pray to God about what to do about the situation. Well, my car did get fixed but as I prayed and cried out to him mad and sad, frustrated all at once, He didn't speak to me about my car, He gave me a prophecy, He spoke to me about my son. He said these exact words "your son is going to be successful" and He
~~~~~~~~~~~~~~~~~~~~~~~~~~~~~~~~~

showed me his face. At that time, I think he was doing paperwork for the Army or Air Force or one of the branches of the military, trying to figure out which way he should go in life. He has been successful despite all life challenges. (2011)

~~~~~~~~~~~~~~~~~~~~~~~~~~~~~~~~~~

A business, when owned, is a lot of responsibility, I remember a time that I prayed to God very specifically about finances, I had a lot on my plate, recently divorced, a small child, head of household and taking care of all of that and then also a business with employees and all the overhead for that. I probably will never forget the 2 rents, 2 light bills, 3 phone lines and 4-5 websites and all expenses for two places. That may be why I'm kind of on the frugal side today. I remember all the expenses put out for 13 years. But I prayed specifically this "God I want $10,000 sitting in the bank, not for bills just sitting in my bank account." I called a friend and told him the prayer that I prayed to God. Well, some months went by, 2 or 3, and during this time (for me God seem to show up most mightily in devastating times also) I
~~~~~~~~~~~~~~~~~~~~~~~~~~~~~~~~~~

was between a rock and a hard place, putting the pieces back together, trying to keep my mind on God, taking trips to restore peace and tranquility in my life and it did keep me. Now we know that the bible says faith without works is dead, so I started praying and thinking of ways to help sustain my business. God allowed me to partner with companies and provide services for their consumers and there were several checks, THEY TOTALED OVER $11,000 *and yes sitting in my bank account just like I prayed, over $10,000. I was so busy working at the time to accommodate all the business that I had forgot the prayer that I had prayed. But my friend reminded me,* REMEMBER THAT PRAYER YOU PRAYED! *When we pray and believe God, our answered prayers cause others to increase their faith and trust in God. (2013)*

~~~~~~~~~~~~~~~~~~~~~~~~~~~~~~~~~~~

I had a horrible dream that one of my family members had raped me. A few days later a vision of the same dream came again. This disturbed me, as this hadn't happened in my real life. We know that dreams
~~~~~~~~~~~~~~~~~~~~~~~~~~~~~~~~~~~

come from God, from the devil and the bible says some dreams we cause ourselves to dream, Jeremiah 29:8. I'm not sure why this dream came to me, but I remember my solution, it was prayer! I prayed and prayed some more rebuking the devil off my life and I prayed for my family member too, nothing but an attack from the enemy to trip me and get off course. The enemy wants to demolish you, guard your hearts and minds. (2016)

~~~~~~~~~~~~~~~~~~~~~~~~~~~~~~

One of the kids had asked me for something, I don't remember what it was, but I felt so bad that I couldn't do it. So, I went to the Lord in desperation, spilling out my hurt feelings in prayer not with a cute little prayer, crying out to Him, pouring my whole heart into the prayer. I do remember telling God I want to be able to fulfill any need my child has, and my heart was heavy about it. Before I could even get off my knees good, I'm kidding not, maybe 3-5 minutes, my phone rung and a lady was very sure about a service even though I had never spoken to her, I talked with her on the phone awhile and she decided to get it, but she did what most don't do,
~~~~~~~~~~~~~~~~~~~~~~~~~~~~~~

she came and placed $500 cash in my hand in a matter of an hour or two, the other $400 she provided a few days later. The entire payment for the whole service in advance. God answered my prayer. When she got there, I was still filled with the spirit from praying and I told her she was the answer to a prayer that I literally just got off my knees praying. We stood and cried together. God does answer and He does it speedily at times. I learned to keep God in my business and to talk about Him with clients even when it felt uncomfortable. (2017)

~~~~~~~~~~~~~~~~~~~~~~~~~~~~~~~~~

I stayed before the Lord praying and studying and seeking His face hours and hours at a time and God would give me sermons very specific, scriptures, and points with it. I had a book of sermons before I even went to ministry school, I still have this book, from early on God was trying to show me what He wanted me to do. Although at the beginning I didn't feel qualified, I couldn't deny any longer, because He continued to give me things and guide me and does so even now. I'm sure, they will be used at some point. Although back then I
~~~~~~~~~~~~~~~~~~~~~~~~~~~~~~~~~

didn't believe that He would call someone like me, I would write down what He gave me. I plan to save all the books for my children and their children.

~~~~~~~~~~~~~~~~~~~~~~~~~~~~~~~~~~~

God kept trying to put my focus back on Him, on the course He already had, so as I took the situation to Him, He never answered what I asked but said these words clearly, " it's not about you, there are people way worse than you, get up and find the biggest pot you can find and feed the homeless, I did just that and that started this ministry. It's been over a decade, and we are still feeding the homeless and added serving and ministering to the women at the shelter.

The first time I went I sat on the ground and ate with them, I've seen people with nothing laying on a wet ground like it was a bed and prayed for hundreds of people and a woman that had fresh black and blue bruises on her face, she said a girl beat her up, even during Covid I had to lay hands on her, as I hugged her and cried with her and I let her know you can make it out of this. Little did I know what God was trying to
~~~~~~~~~~~~~~~~~~~~~~~~~~~~~~~~~~~

get me to do even though we were blessing them, they blessed me in a sense, I found great pleasure from it. Don't ignore the people in your life that been around you for years, sometimes they can see things that you can't see, no matter the cost, focus on God's plan. (2009)

~~~~~~~~~~~~~~~~~~~~~~~~~~~~~~~~

I started praying specifically to God about what some may see as rejected people, that person with a tattoo on their face, or 10 body pierces, prostitutes, alcoholics, drug addicts & dealers, people that some may see as unusable but real Christians know God can clean up anybody. I know some Preachers and Christians with these testimonies. He without sin, cast the first stone. I asked God to give me encounters with these types of people. *OF COURSE, HE ANSWERED THIS PRAYER. I ran into a lady, the one thing I remember is how beautiful she was on the outside, her makeup was on 10, she was dressed so pretty, but there was another side to her, and she opened up to me and it was my key to minister to her. She kept referencing her prison bracelet even though I was just making small talk with her, in*
~~~~~~~~~~~~~~~~~~~~~~~~~~~~~~~~

which I never even saw it, as if she was beating herself up for her mistakes. God will give you discernment and understanding to share a word for the exact person who needs to hear it. I ministered to her "you are not your past or your mistakes, that doesn't define who you are", she was hurting on the inside but looked so good on the outside, so much like many of us, we hide the scars and the hurt. There is help. I prayed for her, encouraged her, invited her to watch the streaming for the church because she had to be in the house because of parole and couldn't be out at night. God will give you the opportunity to help those you are praying for because God wants to deliver His people that are bound and He's going to do it through you. (2018)

~~~~~~~~~~~~~~~~~~~~~~~~~~~~~~~~~~~

I asked God to remove specific desires from my life, back in my younger days I use to drink socially, we would go out in groups and my drink was a margarita with no salt on the realm. I was a social drinker, and we would go out to the clubs on weekdays and weekends. I didn't have a drink until after I graduated high school
~~~~~~~~~~~~~~~~~~~~~~~~~~~~~~~~~~~

and never have, I done drugs. I was raised in the church and went to church a lot when I was a little girl and most my life. My Great Grandfather was a Pastor, and we have a family church. But partying and drinking goes hand and hand. I personally think that alcohol or drugs makes you do and say things you normally wouldn't as well as change your brain cells. I base this on people I have seen and my own experiences, as I'm not a doctor. However, I don't look down on other people's struggles. God took away the desires I prayed to Him about and I don't miss none of it. Take it to God with your whole heart in prayer. (2014)

~~~~~~~~~~~~~~~~~~~~~~~~~~~~~~~~~~~

I was going through a rough season in my marriage, I was praying to God about everything, and He showed me a dream, He never answered the questions I asked but He showed me my husband face at the time and he was preaching in the pulpit. God reveals what He wants to be revealed and answers the way He desires. Your agenda may not be God's agenda, He's always
~~~~~~~~~~~~~~~~~~~~~~~~~~~~~~~~~~~

right. May this encourage you to take the people in your life to God in prayer. (2015)

~~~~~~~~~~~~~~~~~~~~~~~~~~~~~~~~~~

I had a prophecy, there were police and blue lights, twice I was shown that, then there were footsteps and very specifically I remember black shoes like the kind of boots police wear. We must continually pray that what God reveals and sends to us, ask for wisdom and understanding. Deeper knowledge to take the material He provides and be able to discern it. For what, for who, the more discipline the more discerning, I learned. (2017)

~~~~~~~~~~~~~~~~~~~~~~~~~~~~~~~~~~

Someone shared with me that God showed them 2 businesses for me. Over the years I have asked God to bless so I can focus on Him, have time to study and focus on the things He wants me to do and family first. I have had more than 2 businesses for years now. Pray to God about the desires in your heart to make extra income, business ventures, and the means to make it happen. (2015)

~~~~~~~~~~~~~~~~~~~~~~~~~~~~~~~~~~~~

God gave me a dream and I saw my family members face. I didn't know what was going on in her life, but the next day I reached out, once we made contact, she said "yes, I've been going through" I had already started praying for her when He showed me, but I continued to pray for her. We have to ask God why did You show me and what do You want me to do. But at any rate prayer is always in order. Keep your family in prayer, He wants you to reach them too. (2015)

~~~~~~~~~~~~~~~~~~~~~~~~~~~~~~~~~~~~

One day, I was doing a study on Shaback which means, to praise God with a loud voice, that God led me to. I had never done a study on that before, and I found a study called the 7 Hebrew Words for Praise. I studied them all and they were so powerful to me, so much so I wrote them in the front of my bible. I got to bible study on Wednesday and my Pastor was teaching on The 7 Hebrew Words for Praise the exact same material God gave me and shared with us it would be the new sermon series. (2014)

~~~~~~~~~~~~~~~~~~~~~~~~~~~~~~~~~~~~

I had a prophecy of warning, me and some family was sitting on a loveseat, we get a knock at the door, and she mentioned there was an incident and somebody was hurt. She said it was a group of boys and a car involved, then she showed me some papers and it had my son's name on it and that he had died. I woke up crying and screaming. I talked with him about what I saw and warned him to stay away from certain boys and to think about his life choices. We must cover our children in prayer. The devil wants to destroy us and our seeds; He wants the generational curses to continue and the success of your seeds to be null and void. He is still here and doing good. It did scare me, but it didn't stop me. (2014)

~~~~~~~~~~~~~~~~~~~~~~~~~~~~~~~~~~~~

I had a prophetic dream, and it was scary. I was shown a whirlwind like a tornado, and I was caught up in it. I woke up. Was I drowning in life? Was God warning me that a storm was getting the best of me? Was God warning me to prepare for a storm? I prayed to God, what are You trying to show me? Sometimes we don't always know and so we must ask God for revelation. A relevant scripture did provide some knowledge Proverbs 1:27, Job 38 speaks of whirlwinds also. Sometimes storms and strong winds come for warning to seek cover you may have to go to a basement or a room with no windows. God wants to give us a way of escape in our storms of life. But He has the evacuation plan, the safety plan to get you to safe haven. Pray for protection. (2014)

~~~~~~~~~~~~~~~~~~~~~~~~~~~~~~~~~~~

An overwhelming presence of the Holy Spirit came over me like I had never experienced before. I was sitting in the library studying and an out of body experience came over my physical body. This was the beginning of my encounters with the Holy Spirit. I said I'm cold and put my coat on, then minutes, I said its hot and took the jacket off and interesting scenarios like this happened. From this point forward, I had a very strong presence of the Holy Spirit with me. Then, I prayed and asked God what is this? I now understand it was the
~~~~~~~~~~~~~~~~~~~~~~~~~~~~~~~~~~~

Holy Spirit. This happened after I stopped running all those years and told God "Yes" to my calling. (2015)

~~~~~~~~~~~~~~~~~~~~~~~~~~~~~~~~~~~

I went to my doctor and said if you don't give me something, I'm not gone make it. I was experiencing some very low times because I couldn't understand the things that were happening, why my husband treated me the way he did. She prescribed me a medicine. But I kept praying, I had never taken medication before and so I kept talking to God about it. God was able to build me up enough that I didn't need the medication. I meditated day and night and I kept saying God, I don't think that is your plan for me. I got the prescription and never took the drug. God kept me, I received healing from the GREAT PHYSICIAN through the word of God. Thank You, Jesus! I relied on him morning, noon, and night. Fasting, praying, studying, then more of it and it got me through. This was one of many times I learned how to use God's principles for healing in my life. I am the God that healeth thee. (2009)

~~~~~~~~~~~~~~~~~~~~~~~~~~~~~~~~~~~

God had shown me my calling AGAIN. God did a lot to let me know, YOU! I WANT YOU! After I literally cried out to Him, I will never forget being on my knees, crying with my face in the pillow of the loveseat, it was soaked and wet from my tears, snot dripping and my arms were in pain and I had a full book at work, I got mad at God asking Him "why would you allow this to happen?" Knowing I had no other resources to take care of my needs, I was fussing with God, and mad at Him. He then shows me a vision of me preaching AGAIN! The same thing He showed me the first time but this time I didn't tell Him that He had the wrong one. I said God if this is true, if this is what you want me to do, my answer is YES! This was the first time I truly accepted my calling to preach, He had shown me many years prior. About 10 years. Many answered prayers specifically regarding my calling came after this. God was very instructional. Thank You Father. (2014)

~~~~~~~~~~~~~~~~~~~~~~~~~~~~~~~~~

I prayed to God about some things I really needed understanding about. There were three specific things I
~~~~~~~~~~~~~~~~~~~~~~~~~~~~~~~~~

asked God about, at this time I didn't have a church home, God continued to guide regardless of my feelings at the time. He showed me a dream, it was a church and He showed specific details about the outside of the building and a big white steeple. I still didn't connect the dream, but I ended up visiting a church, the first time I went, the Pastor was preaching on one of the specific things I lifted to God, Hmm ok. I visited a second time, and the Pastor was preaching about one of the other three things I prayed about, now puzzled like God what's happening? Lastly, I visited that church a third time and he was preaching on the last of the three things I prayed about. So now I'm like wow! I then knew this was the church He wanted me at. The first three times of visiting the Pastor was preaching on the specific three things I lifted up to God which no one knew about. This is my church Victorious Praise Fellowship Church. Weeks after I joined God had me turn around to look at the outside of the church which is exactly what He had shown me in the dream. God hears and answers when we pray accordingly to His Will for our lives. (2014)

~~~~~~~~~~~~~~~~~~~~~~~~~~~~~~~

I prayed to God about a book that was a new release, just came out, Purpose Drive Life, this was a long time ago as we know the Author has several variations of this book out now. At this time, I needed direction and I said to God, "I want this book". I went to the Goodwill just browsing around and low and behold this brand newly released book was there for $1 and some change. It blessed my life. I still have this book today. God hears you. Don't stop praying. (2003)

~~~~~~~~~~~~~~~~~~~~~~~~~~~~~~~

I had a Prophetess speak over my life, she said she saw me traveling abroad with my business and gave details. What she revealed I do all of that with my business. I've been to all the major states in the U.S. I will never forget what God has done for me. God will send people to you to guide you in your walk. (2018)

~~~~~~~~~~~~~~~~~~~~~~~~~~~~~~~

My knees buckled under me, and I fell to the ground, this has happened many times and I heard a
~~~~~~~~~~~~~~~~~~~~~~~~~~~~~~~

whisper "get up". I declare you find the strength to keep getting up until He brings you out. (2018)

~~~~~~~~~~~~~~~~~~~~~~~~~~~~~~~~~~~

I was at church and had a need, I can't remember what the need was, but I do remember crying out to God at the altar about it. So, when church was over, I decided to take a backroad home still full of the spirit and as I was driving down the road, I get a call from a young lady, and I had to pull over into a shopping center to take the call. I told her what the price would be for the service around $1,100 and she said great, I didn't want to go over $1,500. God fulfilled the need; it was more than what I needed. Before I could even make it home GOD HAD ANSWERED MY PRAYER! God is concerned with all parts of our lives even our finances. Never underestimate your cries to the Lord. God promises where 2 or 3 are in the mist, I will be also; He cares about your circumstances and will deliver but it may not happen exactly the way you think it should. Remember God is the architect, let Him stay in charge. (2016)

~~~~~~~~~~~~~~~~~~~~~~~~~~~~~~~~~~~

Before my calling, I served a lot: Feeding the homeless, going to nursing homes, singles ministry leader, door greeter, teenage Sunday school teacher, singles bible study, singing and choir rehearsal, youth ministry called Roots of Ruth for young girls and more. One day God showed me a dream and I was in the pulpit, and I was preaching. I prayed to God, "You don't know me, You got the wrong one" and I continued to say that to Him. At the time I was ashamed, not someone like me. Although at the time I was puzzled, I never stopped praying about it, I said "God send me to someone I can talk to about it". I never shared what He showed me with anyone. God never stopped letting me know what He wanted me to do. After this prayer I prayed to Him, He showed me the face of a person: I respected her, a deaconess, she was holy, humble, and a faithful woman of God. I always admired her, she showed great faith, spiritual maturity, we also sung together. He answered my prayer "send me to someone I can talk to about it" but I avoided His answer to my prayer and some more time went by, I never went to her because I felt I was unworthy to be used by God, at least in my eyes. Well, she came to me and said I need to talk to you. We went for breakfast, and she shared that God had shown her a dream about me and I was preaching in the pulpit, the same dream He had shown me. After this confirmation I still didn't accept it until years later. Now I know, I'm just right to be used by Him, handpicked by God. (2006)

~~~~~~~~~~~~~~~~~~~~~~~~~~~~~~~~

I walked away from a man that proposed, a man of God that loves the Lord and he was raised to be such. I remember how amazing his mom and dad was, a great example of a Christian family. I loved him and he loved me, "my high school sweetheart". I dated him all my high school years, but once I graduated, I moved away. I turned away to that which I was never raised to be, by that I mean hanging out and hanging with people that were up to no good leash on life, I hope this speaks to someone. Most of my life, all I knew was church. At 18/19 yrs. old, I started partying, drinking, and made decisions that were not intended for my life. This was a costly mistake. as I'm pleading to young people right
~~~~~~~~~~~~~~~~~~~~~~~~~~~~~~~~

now, God knew what I needed, if I would have stayed on His path then, a lot of things would not have happened. I had relationships that were not pleasing to God, I didn't follow what He designed for me, I felt like I was dealt a bad hand in life but looking back some of it was derived from bad choices I made at a young age, like this one, some were generational curses. I would have avoided a lot of heartache, pain, and tough times. The choices made at a time in life can end up being choices you have to live with for life. (1995)

~~~~~~

I had 3 miscarriages, I didn't understand why, I've always been health conscious. My family use to call me the food police, so I started crying out to God. I felt so many of times like David in his prayer, Psalms 22: 1; My God, my God, why hast thou forsaken me? Why art thou so far from helping me, 2 O my God, I cry in the daytime, but thou hearest not; and in the night season and am not silent." Look at how David cried out to God, sounds very familiar to me, the times I have cried out to him in my own personal prayer time and at church, just
~~~~~~

letting it all go to get His attention. Or like Jeremiah, "I am the man who has seen affliction under the rod of God's wrath, 2 He has driven me away and made me walk in darkness instead of light. 3 Indeed, He keeps turning His hand against me all day long".

You don't have to say it; I know some of you have felt this way. Yes, I have felt like Jeremiah, like God had turned against me. But there's something about going to Him in such manner with no agenda, no form, no fashion, humbly, with no cares of what you look like in His presence. He wants us to pour it all out to Him. To me that says ***GOD IM DESPERATE FOR YOU AND YOUR HAND IN MY LIFE****. David even said in the same chapter "I was poured out like water", Psalms 22:14. But I said to God, "have my mistakes caused You to curse my womb? God, are You allowing this to happen because of the way I lived my life and the things in my past? I could have made better decisions; I could have chosen a different way when things came up. I was distraught and thought that God was hindering me because of my past. But God showed me, NOT SO!*

I'm here to tell you even when you feel some type of way about yourself, God does not feel that way about you and He shows his unconditional love and mercy. Mercies are new every morning.

The doctors told me they didn't know if I would be able to carry a baby, they didn't know if it would be normal, or if it would make it, he restricted my travel for business because he was scared, I would go into pre-term deliver. But God not only allowed me to conceive naturally "after" 3 miscarriages, I carried the baby full term, worked throughout my whole pregnancy and welcomed the baby with hearts full of joy of what God had done, a beautiful little girl, my daughter, Hailey. God is so good, *and He is real,* HE IS *A* PRAYER *ANSWERING* GOD, *I speak open wombs in the life of wives alongside their husbands, believing for a family. When the doctors give you a report of infertility, unfavorable test results, health statistics, whose report will you believe? (2010)*

~~~~~~~~~~~~~~~~~~~~~~~~~~~~~~~~
~~~~~~~~~~~~~~~~~~~~~~~~~~~~~~~~

I had been praying to God to give me opportunity to witness to the unsaved and challenged. I walked up to the bus stop and there was a man with a beer in his hand. I said a general hello, nothing more. I knew he was an experienced drinker because I smelt the alcohol coming out of his skin and he had physical signs. He didn't know but I was praying for him. He said to me. I know God too. Keep in mind I never spoke to him about God or church. I said the same God who help me to get over my struggles is the same God that can help you lay that down. I never saw him again. The God in you shows even without you saying a word. When we go to witness to others, we must make sure we do it in humility because we were once in sin. (2018)

~~~~~~~~~~~~~~~~~~~~~~~~~~~~~~~~~~~

I took a lunch break and drove to get food, as I was leaving, I got in my right-hand lane to leave, an 18-wheeler transfer truck, instead of pulling behind me, the trucker came on the left side of me and made a right-hand turn, like I was not waiting to turn. He flipped my car over in a deep ditch that was right beside the street.
~~~~~~~~~~~~~~~~~~~~~~~~~~~~~~~~~~~

He never stopped to see if me and my unborn child was ok. But thank God we suffered no injuries. To God be all the glory for His protection. (1996)

~~~~~~~~~~~~~~~~~~~~~~~~~~~~~~~~

I experienced a horrible marriage that left me asking God many questions. This life obstacle made me feel like there was nothing keeping me here. I was devastated and I wanted to check out. Although I had money, a successful business at the time, it still didn't ease the hurt. So, I rented a Lexus truck and drove to VA, on my drive there from NC I said Lord, I wonder what it feels like to run into the ocean. I wanted to check out of life. I rented a hotel room and locked myself in there for days. But I had enough God in me after several days of being suicidal to remind myself that I am loved, my life has purpose, and God allowed me to make it through another test. God is a restorer, He heals, He can raise you up, He can fill you and make you feel whole again. He will save you from destruction and remind you of His promises. Money nor fame can save you, only Jesus. (2010)
~~~~~~~~~~~~~~~~~~~~~~~~~~~~~~~~

~~~~~~~~~~~~~~~~~~~~~~~~~~~~~~~~~~~

God spoke to me and said clear as day, "What are you waiting for, I've given you everything you need?" Right when you think God will turn His back to you, He will run to you with open arms to scoop you up from drowning in your own self-pity, pick you up off the floor, then an inner voice says get up, a whisper in your ear. I was not thinking about ministering or preaching again at the time, but God was, this was my favorite line "see God, I told you I was the wrong one", but not so. Some people may see you as your mistake, but God doesn't. My answer in response was: "You shoal is right", God and started going to Him about what He would put my hands to. I started ministering and serving more, added the women shelter and started consulting Him on what more He wanted me to do. (2019)

~~~~~~~~~~~~~~~~~~~~~~~~~~~~~~~~~~~

A prophetess came to our church and said anyone with wrist issues, come up. I had carpal tunnel for years and would have severe pain. She laid hands on my wrist, and I haven't missed another day's work since then over wrist pain. Before I would have to cancel my books until my hands stopped hurting. (2017)

~~~~~~~~~~~~~~~~~~~~~~~~~~~~~~~~

God gave me a dream after I went to Him about myself. He showed me walking down a path. As I got closer a person was standing there, In the dream the person said to me, "your grandma said it was this". (2016)

~~~~~~~~~~~~~~~~~~~~~~~~~~~~~~~~

I was praying and I heard God say to me "just do good". It's so easy to clap back at people who may come for you, and if we choose to do that, in their minds they think it validates, "see I told you she ain't saved", but I learned how to rest in God and let Him handle it or do it in a manner pleasing to God. (2019)

~~~~~~~~~~~~~~~~~~~~~~~~~~~~~~~~

God gave me a dream after I cried out to him in desperation. I wasn't sure which way to go and what to do, but I knew God knew about it all. So, I prayed to God about the gentlemen so that he could lead me and tell me what was really the truth. I was very specific here
~~~~~~~~~~~~~~~~~~~~~~~~~~~~~~~~

again in the prayer, praying only for the situation. God showed me his face and the woman's face I had questioned many times before and additional information I was seeking was given from God. Giving me the facts that I needed to decide. What God reveals is the truth. (2020)

~~~~~~~~~~~~~~~~~~~~~~~~~~~~~~~~~~~~~~

God spoke to me about ministering, I wrote down what I felt the people in the world need from me, what I had to give based on the testimonies and experiences God had given me. I prayed to God about it and He spoke to me very clearly these words, WHEN YOU GO THROUGH THE FIRE. *I knew it was a scripture. When I got to the scripture it was describing the same information that I had wrote but I didn't have a scripture down, a conference that minister to women, this is the Deliver Me from Myself Conference, God gave to help deliver others. God also confirmed it, a wise woman, old enough to be my grandma, called me and said God gave me a word for you and it was the exact scripture God had given me. She ministered to me and*
~~~~~~~~~~~~~~~~~~~~~~~~~~~~~~~~~~~~~~

said don't stop nothing you're doing, God is gonna use you to minister to certain women. (2019)

~~~~~~~~~~~~~~~~~~~~~~~~~~~~~~~~~~~

I have a great wise woman in my life, before I would leave her presence she would cover me in prayer, she would talk with me on the phone and would pray before we were off, I purposely watched her life. She freely shared her testimony that I would have never known she went through such stuff. I went to her one day and wanted to share with her what was going on but was ashamed. However, God revealed the exact thing that I was going to bring to her, and she ministered to me. We need people we can go to, wise and godly at all times. (2019)

~~~~~~~~~~~~~~~~~~~~~~~~~~~~~~~~~~~

I needed to pay my school tuition and got up the day of class, still unpaid. I reminded God about the scripture that if I asked anything according to His Will, He hears us, and we know we have what we petition. I called my professor and he said to come to class anyway. Before I could sit down good, I got a cash app notice on my phone and a customer saying she wanted to go ahead and prepay for her service, and it was more than my tuition. God is good and He will provide for you, 30,60,100-fold, according to His will, He planned for your life. (2019)

~~~~~~~~~~~~~~~~~~~~~~~~~~~~~~~~

Laying quiet before the Lord and I heard Him say, "I'm not only concerned with your spiritual success, but success in all". God has without a doubt manifested blessing in all parts of my life. (2019)

~~~~~~~~~~~~~~~~~~~~~~~~~~~~~~~~

I remember one specific time that changed my life. God kept placing a young lady in my spirit, He showed me a vision of her face and I kept putting it off, several times he did this 3 or 4 times. I finally reached out weeks later and when I called her, her mom had passed, and I was so hard on myself for not reaching out when God first told me to. I believe God knew she needed someone to be there for her in that time of grief. From that time moving forward I learned that when God place people in ones' spirit I either write it down so I can get to them at my first free time, or I go ahead and contact them.

~~~~~~~~~~~~~~~~~~~~~~~~~~~~~~~~~~~

In conclusion of this chapter, the faith and strength seen in some people, a lot of times came from their experiences with God. I'm now at a place with God that nothing can change my mind, turn me away, stop me from doing His Will and purpose. Nothing can stop my praise or shut my mouth because of my experiences with Him. He has changed my life and for the rest of my life, come what may, I give Him my praise, time, resources, and all I had to give. I challenge you to pray to God about your relationship with Him. Ask Him to draw you closer and to show you His power in your life, to give you signs and wonders. Pray and ask God to look on behalf of your personal needs and what obstacles that lay before you. Don't let any challenges hinder you from God or what He told you to do. Ask God to speak to you, Tell God you want to experience Him on a different level. I pray that He gives you just as many experiences as He has given me.

^^
~~~~~~~~~~~~~~~~~~~~~~~~~~~~~~~~~~~

" We may see our work as our careers but then I learned how to share God at work and when I did so I noticed God specifically sending ppl that need him maybe a closer walk or need to be witnessed to. God sent a pk kid to me who was gay, God sent a young lady who was a traveling nurse; her mom was an elder and others. God sent me clients that needed him. Our callings are not just for church work and at spiritual functions. The times I brought God into the conversation " ONLY THEN " DID THEY OPEN UP. I pray God give you bold faith to talk about His goodness and be not ashamed because they seem unreceptive. One broke down in tears and found out she had just lost her fiancée. I cried with her and prayed for her. Your calling does spill into your career even though our REAL CAREERS IS WINNING SOULS.... HE SENDS WHO HE DESIRES TO SEND TO WHAT WE SEE AS OUR CAREERS TO SAVE SOULS; HE SENDS US TO LET THEM KNOW " MY CHILD I HAVENT FORGOTTEN YOU. IN MY OPINION THOSE I ENCOUNTERED FELT. "

LEFT BEHIND" Be ready to share God at work, ball game, restaurant. Anywhere, Anytime, Amen?

Notes:

Chapter 4

Situational Prayers

Sometimes we need that special person we can call on and they know you so well you don't need to ask for prayer, but they can sense it just from listening. We younger women learn from those who are wiser and older, and I can't tell you how many times I went to Godly women, and they helped me in my life to be who I am today. They all poured into me freely, with open arms, very giving and I so needed that. Pray to God about what you need, some was sent, the others I sought after. But getting what you need is important to completing the task God puts in your hands. When you get in the presence of a spirit filled man or woman of God it's like your favorite blanket you cuddle with. God can reveal to them what to say to you. This happens with clients too, they would say, "God said give you this", and it would be 2x, 3x the amount, $100, $200 tips. God is good and will blow you mind. Just be open and willing. The willing and obedient shall eat the fruit of the land, Isiah 1:19.

Reaching God Through Your Prayers

In this chapter there are a few prayers that may help lead you in your own prayers. After each prayer there's a section to write how you feel, how He may speak to you, or what God lays on your heart. What do you want to declare, confess? What do you want to share with God? There's also a section called: "my next step", to jot down what He brings to you, what next moves He may be leading you to take:

- ***Self-Prayer***
- ***Discipline Prayer***
- ***Family Prayer***
- ***Suicidal Prayer***
- ***Depression Prayer***
- ***Self-Declaration Prayer***
- ***Spouse Prayer***
- ***Desperate Prayer***
- ***Self-Help Prayer***
- ***Sacrificial Prayer***
- ***Enemies Prayer***

- ***Singles Prayer***
- ***Peace Prayer***
- ***Healing Prayer***
- ***Salvation Prayer***

Self-Prayer

The biggest prayer you will pray will remain to be the prayer you pray to work on yourself. A lot of times we must step back from situations and get before the Lord. Sometimes it's good to just sit in His presence and hear from Him.

Jesus said: "Deny yourself, take up your cross and follow me", Matthew 16:24. This is suggesting, if I may paraphrase, you can't be centered around yourself and serve God; denying yourself, your desires and will, your flesh, what you think, what you want, what you want to say, what you may want to do; ***SELFLESSNESS***. Jesus served.

I can't even begin to count the numerous of times I've had to go to God and say to God "work on me Lord", "work on my mind God", "I even said, God what's wrong with me". I've had to say "God help me to do this" etc., countless, and countless prayers for myself alone. There is so much that falls in this category, it could be time and money to go to school or a big one for me and maybe for others is the selfless daily acts for our kids. For most parents this is normal.

Talking about self, God help me to share this in a way that will help somebody. I remember times when I kept seeing the same things pop up. Now when we have humbled ourselves and we're sitting in prayer with God, we stop turning it on others and shine the light on us, we take the magnifying glass and position it directly on ourselves. "God is it me? Show me what I'm doing wrong. God is it something in me?" I have asked God many times, "God show me my weakness, show me the things I need to grow in". Help me to focus on me, the errors in me, my own flaws, and the things I need to work on more than the short comings I see in others.

Prayer:

God I'm standing in the need of prayer, work on me. I've done things I shouldn't have done; I've said things I shouldn't have said, sometimes I don't respond in the right way, help me, forgive me. Fill my heart, my mind, my soul, my mouth, with your goodness. God, break down our self-barriers and turmoil's, free our mind and give us the tools to do it, keep our mind on the things it should be on, In Jesus Name. God give strength to labor in the word and replay what You've said to us or what Your word says if that's what it takes in the time of what we may be going through, so that it can keep us and deliver us. I rebuke the devil from our desires and things we may want to do to make us a better person. Passions we have of doing good and the goals we have in life, all we aspire to be, God; fill us with more of Your Spirit, hear our cries Lord and not only hear but respond. We wanna be more like You, don't turn Your face from us. Answer our cries. Let our goodness far outweigh. Your word says the good I want to do, I don't and the evil I shouldn't do, that I do, Romans 7:19. Help us God! Be pleased with our lives, may we bring You glory. Forgive us for wrongs, help us to make it right, we repent before You Lord. In Jesus Name, Amen.

My personal confession(s)

My next steps:

Discipline Prayer

This area is very important for Christians and new believers alike, as we must learn to bring things under subjection and discipline our lifestyle. Most people who have been around me know I'm a talker. I used to tell people if you see me in a corner quiet, something is definitely wrong. I still can say quite a bit when I get going but I learned also that there are times when I need to be quiet; maybe to listen, maybe to observe, to hear what God may want to say or what the Holy Spirit may be nudging one to do. I also used to binge watch shows for hours I'm talking about like 5 to 6 hours, spending an entire evening just doing so. I used to go to one of my favorite restaurants for a large, sweet tea almost daily until I had to learn to break away from things that may hinder my walk, harm my health, keep me from the closeness that was needed, the oneness with God. As I grew in God my desires changed also. Many years ago, I did a fast from television and I have not sat, and binge watched television like that since then. I don't watch TV that much now. No, I didn't get rid of my tea but only occasionally I have it, I still love sweet tea, that's the country girl in me. We must discipline everything about us. The way we think, our mouths, what we do, what we watch, what we spend our money on, our desires, the places we go and the people we entertain, all need to be disciplined. I still must pray and ask God to help me. When we discipline our lives, we see changes and it trickles down into other areas of our life, reminding one of what to keep as priority. If we are going to be anything for God, God working through us, discipline will be required.

Prayer:

Father I pray that You give us wisdom and examine our lives. Help us to discern in areas that we may need change, break off things that are not like You Father. Remove distractions and things that keep us busy, so busy that we don't have time that's required with You. Give us a hunger and thirst to grow in the things of You. Break away worldliness, break away all ungodly relationships and unwholesome talk that the bible says leads to ungodliness, 2 Timothy 2:16. God sweep through our homes, our churches, and fill them with the things of You, the fruits of the Spirit. Show us the results of having discipline in our homes and churches, the fruit from doing so and let our family, our communities, our spouses, our churches and of course our lives reap the benefits. In Jesus Name, Amen.

My personal confession(s):

My next steps:

Family Prayer

Family can be best described as those who are in your corner, a body of people with togetherness, a closeness in mind and spirit with one. Those who help see you through the good and the bad. Sometimes family for some people are not those in their blood family. Some have extended family and friends. But whatever your family structure looks like you find positivity, support, and love that is unconditional. Covering our family in prayer is what we are called to do. In the bible there are many examples of family and what it should be like but unfortunately there are also examples of how family attacks and curses are present and how families should not behave. Joseph's brothers who left him in a dungeon to die all because of jealousy, Genesis 37. Job's wife who told him he should curse God and die, Job 2. Cain who murdered his brother Abel, Genesis 4, and we know there are many ways of murder other than just physical killing. Some families murdered their family's character or broke their spirits and caused them a mental or emotional death, God help us. Also, on the contrary: family, whatever that looks like for you can be a blessing. I had a lot of great women that shaped, molded, deposited in me, helped me and they are family. There is also in the bible the father who celebrated the return of his son in Luke 15. The word explains how by obedience, attacks and generational curses can cease, Deuteronomy 30: 1-20, 29:22-29.

When we have family members for whatever reason that don't go to God in prayer, we should step in on their behalf and intercede. Prayer is always in order. It could be just what saves them. As we never know what seed was planted that grew in their hearts and minds, but God knows. One waters, one plants, but God increases it, 1 Corinthians 3:7. That may even be the reason God called you in the first place. Maybe He called you to reach your family, Amen.

Prayer:

Father I lift my family up to You first and foremost, (insert family members), my children, mother, father, brothers, sister, aunts, uncles, cousins. I pray that You be with them Lord, protect them everywhere they go, bring them closer to You Lord. God, I pray that You would make my family stronger and to help us to love and support each other. Strengthen us individually and then strengthen our family as a whole. Bless my family, heal what's not like You, set us free from strongholds, weaknesses, desires, generational curses passed down and let them know how much You love them. Speak to them, tear down the works of the enemy that tries to enter in and kill family structure. God's order, of a mom and a dad in homes, count the cost of family togetherness. Grow us in Your word, for this is what matures us; how we know when somethings the right way or not the right way: the word is our guide on living right and how we should treat each other. Give us strong faith, believing fully. Father I pray for families abroad. Take mothers, fathers, brothers, sisters, aunts, uncles, cousins, and strengthen family bonds. Heal brokenness, restore love in homes, I speak hardness of hearts removed in the name of Jesus. I speak what generational curses that came before us are no longer, in Jesus' name. I speak healing in the lives of family and restoration of families, a release of peace and restoration of joy in the name of Jesus. I speak blessings in the lives of families, I speak right now that (insert your family) will be what each other need to make it, in Jesus' name. I speak that families: my family, your family shall live and not die because we pray for each other. Help us to forgive one another for all have sinned and falling short of your glory. God, we want You to be pleased with our lives and how to conduct ourselves even in our family. So, speak to us, show us the right way to do things. Keep family bonds strong, intact, break curses for our children's children. Help us to love with a big spoon not a measuring spoon keeping up with who did what and removing it, here and there, as Your love never runs out on us, Romans 8:35. God we can only do this in Your strength. Help us to do so, in Jesus Name. We love and bless Your Holy Name for all You have done, Amen.

My personal confession(s):

My next steps:

Suicidal Prayer

Who has ever prayed "God take my life", or "I don't see a reason for living, "God take me away from all of this", or what I said to God, "I don't see why you are keeping me here"! There is hope, God is attentive to the cries of His children. I remember being in a dark place. I was doing so good; I had a business and was looking at buildings to open a 2nd location. I was traveling all around the world with my businesses making over 100k one year, flying to Miami, LA, Dallas, and NY regularly, doing clients, booming salon 10 employees and teaching. I had 5 instructors in my education firm, teaching in 3 states and then I got in a strange season. I noticed the decline after the marriage, now looking back. The blessings of the Lord maketh rich and addeth no sorrow, Proverbs 10:22. Blessing is not just money but favor and protection on our life. The problems were from the start. I ignored the signs. It seems like my business, my finances, like everything went downhill. I went to see a therapist and I told her I didn't see a reason for being there. Within our session, the therapist started crying with me, I had family curses & dilemmas from an early age, a horrible spouse & marriage, things in life were declining, I felt like I had no one, no one I could depend on in times of trouble or weakness, no one in my corner to help, no one to pick me up when I fell or got down. But shout this; BUT GOD!!!!

THE DEVIL WILL ALWAYS MAKE THINGS LOOK WORSE THAN THEY ARE! I KNOW THAT NOW, HE WILL PLANT THINGS IN YOUR HEAD THAT ARE NOT TRUE, HE WILL MAKE YOU SAY THINGS THAT YOU WISH YOU WOULD NOT HAVE SAID, HE WILL HAVE YOU FEELING A CERTAIN WAY FOR NO REASON, OR MAYBE THERE WAS A REASON. BUT ITS NOT UNTO DEATH TO TAKE YOUR LIFE THAT GOD ALREADY CALLED BLESSED. THE DEVIL

BLOWS THINGS UP, MANGIFIES THINGS. I KNOW THE DEVILS TACTICS NOW.

God restored me, God never left, and blessing season came again, but there had to be some purging. The job offers and the salary got bigger and bigger, the favor got bigger and bigger, Celebrities calling me to do services and people of high regard. I asked God how did they find little ole me? Teaching opportunities in Chicago and Las Vegas; I asked her why she chose me, the only African American teacher on the roster with a sold-out class 200+. Blessings! Business increasing but this time it seems like it was people who needed God, they were successful in life but not spiritually. God sent PK kids, some had parents that were Elders. My God! But the biggest of all is the work He did in me. He healed my mind, He gave me peace, He restored me and filled me with goodness. He kept letting me know I will never leave, I will never cast you away, I'm the one you can always count on. He sent me people that loved and supported me, more than what I needed. Now, over a decade ago, during that time, I was a Christian, and I loved the Lord but sometimes we can allow situations to overtake us instead of *US OVERTAKING THE SITUATION. WE HAVE BEEN GIVEN ALL THE POWER WE NEED TO GET OVER, TO MAKE IT, TO OVER COME ANY OBSTACLES THAT COME OUR WAY. WITH GOD YES! ALONE NO!*

So, when people reach out to me, I always say find a church home or I'll connect them to someone because if the devil get you alone by yourself, you start to say it don't matter if I'm here or not, there is nothing for me, I see all these people with purpose and dreams and doing great things and I don't see any of that for myself. But God! That is for you. That is, you. You have purpose, your life has purpose, you have desires; ashes may be covering them up from where you've been beat down by life and it got darker and darker. Situations snatched your hope, doomed you and it shrunk you down, maybe the darkness is from family and those close, people you associate with. Dark clouds following you and it seems like no matter where you turn, they follow you everywhere you go. But the devil is a liar, God makes beauty out of ashes, Isaiah 61:3. He will polish you and have you shining bright. Let Your light so shine that they may see Your good works and glorify God, Matthew 5:16-18. Yes, you may have had some tough times, you may have been through a rough patch, maybe you were guilty of it. You just need support; you just need a team. You just need some help; you just need some encouragement. You just need someone that genuinely cares, then most of all we must allow God to build us up. Thank you, Father. I have been there, and God had to do a lot of work on me.

Say this:

I am a mighty woman or man of God; God is my strength and my portion. God is a present need and help when the waves come crashing. He will throw out the life jacket to save me. I will do great things for God; my life has purpose and God is gonna use me.

God, I thank you that You took my name (insert name) and before You formed me, *YOU CREATED MY LIFE PLAN*, Jeremiah 1:5. Through the years, somewhere along the way things got shifted. *GOD SHIFT ME BACK ON COURSE, PUT ME BACK ON TRACK, TURN ME BACK TO YOU, BACK TO THE PLAN YOU DESIGNED FOR MY LIFE FROM THE VERY BEGINNING.*

I SPEAK VICTORY IN THE LIFE OF (INSERT NAME). YOU WILL BE GREAT, YOU WILL BE ALL THAT GOD CREATED YOU TO BE, SAY: GOD WILL HELP ME TO FOCUS, GOD WILL HELP ME TO STAND WHEN I WANT TO GIVE UP, GOD WILL FIGHT MY BATTLES FOR ME, GOD WILL UPHOLD ME WITH HIS WORD. HELP ME TO PUT ON THE WHOLE ARMOR OF GOD SO I CAN

WITHSTAND THESE TRIALS, THESE CIRCUMSTANCES THAT ARE TRYING TO OVERTAKE MY MIND, MY LIFE. I SHALL LIVE. I HAVE MANY REASONS TO LIVE. GOD SEND PEOPLE INTO MY LIFE TO BUILD ME UP AND HELP ME TO ENCOURAGE MYSELF ALSO. I SHALL LIVE, I WILL MAKE IT, I'LL OVERCOME WHATS TRYING TO OVERCOME ME, I'LL HAVE PEACE IN MY MIND, I'LL SAY WHAT GOD SAYS ABOUT ME AND YOU SAID I'LL BLESS YOUR GOING OUT AND COMING IN, I'LL MAKE YOU THE HEAD AND NOT THE TAIL, I'LL MAKE YOU A LENDER AND NOT A BORROWER. I'LL NEVER LEAVE NOR WILL I EVER FORSAKE YOU, AND MY LOVE WILL NEVER LEAVE, AMEN.

In the Name of Jesus, I ask a special blessing on the person reading this prayer, I ask that You fill them with an abundance of peace and joy, love and wisdom. Let them know how much You care for them. God, we honor You for what You're going to do in the life of the person reading this, we thank You in advance. Go live your best life, in Jesus Name, Amen. 1 Peter 5:7, Cast all your cares upon Him, for He careth for you.

My personal confession(s):

My next steps:

Depression Prayer

Unrest in the mind is not God's way for our life. Depression in any part is different from what God says about us; as a man thinketh, so is he, Proverbs 23:7. So we can cause manifestation of a thing just because we thought that way. We can choose to think thoughts of peace, love, and gratefulness. Whatever things are pure, just, of good report, think on these things, Philippians 4:8.

Some feelings of depression: sadness, anxiety, anger, fear, loneliness, and despair, can be brought upon out of various situations, people, work environments, trauma, etc. However, in all these things they are completely contrary to what God is, what He promises to be for us and how He says we should handle these things. God is joy, peace, power, never leaving and never forsaking. Yes, our minds can go to a sad and depressed state if we allow it, but having done all to stand, Eph 6. Any feelings can be cast down, brought to be removed from the mind and spirit, and replaced with peace, 2 Corinthians 10:5. The word shares a story with us in the old testament, 1 Samuel 16, about Saul: The Spirit of the LORD departed from Saul, and an evil spirit from the LORD troubled him; 15: And Saul's servants said unto him, Behold now, an evil spirit from God troubleth thee; 16: Let our Lord now command thy servants, *which are* before thee, to seek out a man, *who is* a cunning player on a harp: and it shall come to pass, when the evil spirit from God is upon thee, that he shall play with his hand, and thou shalt be well. 19: Wherefore Saul sent messengers unto Jesse, and said, send me David thy son, which *is* with the sheep. 23: And it came to pass, when the *evil* spirit from God was upon Saul, that David took a harp, and played with his hand: so, Saul was refreshed, and was well, and the evil spirit departed from him. Saul received healing through music therapy. Therapy can help whether it be music, a licensed professional or counsel of a pastor. They all will benefit you as it did for me. Let us pray.

Prayer:

God, we bless Your Holy name, we reverence You for who You are, we magnify Your name. Dear Heavenly Father, hear my cries and answer, respond. It's me God, standing in need. Dwell with us, walk with us. God, I thank You for being my savior, I thank You for being my healer, I thank You for keeping me and for saving me, nothing and no one can keep me or deliver me but You O Lord. So, I look to You, I pray to You, I develop a hunger and thirst for You. You are God, my God and I look to You for all my help. I know You are concerned with all parts of me and to be effective in my purpose You have for me, I must be healthy. So, God release anything that's not like You. Fixate my mind on You and Your word, help me to remove things that may be stressors in my life. I declare a life of peace, peace in my home, the friends I surround myself with uplift and encourage, I speak peace in my mind, Lord take the stresses, traumas, frustrations, all those stinking thinking's that the devil sends and replace with peace, love, and joy. Grow us closer to You and keep us near to You. We thank You that we shall live and not die. The devil will not have me, my family, my seed, or anyone connected to me, we will have the victory, in Jesus Name, Amen.

My personal confession(s):

My next steps:

Self-Declaration Prayer

We must speak life over ourselves. Sometimes you must remind yourself and encourage your own self. David encouraged himself in the Lord, 1 Samuel 30:6. Instead of saying I can't do this, speak, and declare success. Get up and get to work at it, setting goals and chipping at the work you have at hand until it's finished. If you have to, post sticky notes on your bathroom mirror to uplift or a saying on your nightstand, whatever it takes. Even when you don't feel like it. Even with obstacles, declare what the Lord has already spoken regarding you. You can find a lot of promises in His word. Amen? I declare over your life, the aspirations and desires, God said I will bless what you put your hands to, God has shown me this many times. Faith without works is dead so if you have a burning desire, start on it, even if you start small. Declare I will get this done. Declare I have all I need within me to do so. Declare I've been given the power to do great things, I, (insert your name), shall do great things and I shall complete all God has put me in charge of.

Prayer:

I shall live and not die; I will become all God has purposed me to be. I will be successful, everything I touch shall be blessed. My body is blessed and in good health. My children are blessed. I rebuke the enemies plans off my life. Anything the devil sends my way will not harm me. My mind will be focused on what I need to do. God will see to the plans He started in me to completion. I will be strong; I will live long and enjoy life. I will complete my goals and business ventures. I will keep the faith and not waver. I will stand strong and see things to the end. I shall make it! I have been given all power to have the victory in every area of my life. I will have victory in my home, in my finances, at work, at my business, in all things I will be victorious. I am the head and not the tail. I will be a blessing to others, I will be a lender and not a borrower. I am the righteousness of God, in Jesus Name, Amen.

My personal confession(s):

My next steps:

Spouse Prayer

God's order of marriage is the right way to do relationships, keeping the blessings on the covenant is important. One of the ways to keep God's blessing on a marriage between (man)one husband and one wife (woman) is by following His word as to how to function in marriage. There are plenty of scriptures that talk about how to love spouses, it even talks about divorce and the way to avoid getting divorced is by not hardening your heart, Matthew 19:8. This is one of many solutions to divorce proof your marriage. I personally believe if two Christ centered and matured people come together that live by the word of God and handle the issues the way God says, you can weather anything. The ability to always communicate in an effective manner and put other's needs, feelings, etc., before your own, ***SELFLESSNESS***, is so important. The word tells us that we shouldn't refrain or hold love, affection from our spouses because it can cause strife, only for prayer and fasting for a limited time, 1 Corinthians 7:5. Singles can pray for their spouse, I heard a person give testimony on how she used to pray about the type of spouse she wanted, she is married now, and he had all those qualities. Let us pray.

Prayer:

Lord, I thank You for my spouse (insert their name). Lord You said in all things give thanks for this is the will of God concerning You. I thank You for giving me a help meet. I ask that You protect my spouse mind God and fill it with Your word. Help them to think on that in all situations and when making choices and decisions. Father strengthen my spouse relationship with You, give them greater faith, an even greater prayer life, give them greater wisdom and knowledge, lead, and guide them in situations regarding our home, our children, our work, our finances, our communication, even our bed Lord, that You said was undefiled. Protect marriages Lord for the devil doesn't want that to succeed either because it glorifies You. God let these marriages be examples of how Christ centered individuals can come together and build a kingdom home that God will bless. Lord I honor my spouse (insert their name), I rededicate my life to them, my time, my heart, my love. Heal any and all hurt and help us to do it Your way moving forward. Devil we speak to you also as the word says you roam the earth seeking whom you may devour. Don't allow the devil to destroy when circumstances arise, I cast down sickness, as we vowed in sickness and in health, I cast down unemployment and lack of money, finances and resources as the vow is for rich or for poor. I pray God that You bless marriages, let that man and that woman follow You with their whole heart individually and then collectively. Cover and sustain marriages, keep families together, breaking the curses in covenants. Amen. Lord we lift this pray in Your son Jesus Name, Amen.

My personal confession:

My next steps:

Desperate Prayer

Someone once said that desperate times calls for desperate measures. In Mark 9:29 (NLT) says: Jesus replied, "This kind can be cast out only by prayer and fasting."

Sometimes obstacles come our way and it feels like you're gonna be destroyed, like you won't be able to take it. Because let's be clear the devil is trying to kill you. *HE IS TRYING TO GET YOU TO DRIVE OVER THE BRIDGE, HE IS TRYING TO GET YOU TO LEAVE YOUR SPOUSE, HE IS TRYING TO GET YOU TO PUMP SO MANY DRUGS AND ALCOHOL IN YOUR BODY THAT IT LEAVES YOU LIFELESS. JESUS! HE IS TRYING TO DEMOLISH YOU!* The devil comes to kill, steal, and destroy, John 10:10. So, the way to survive during devastating times is to be full, be prepared. Full of God, Full of the Spirit, Spiritual things. because that is what will keep you. NOT STUFF! Let God soothe you. Let Him lead you as what to do next. a 2-way communication system, allowing the word to seep deep in you so that you understand and change can take place, breaking down the words in a verse and maybe you meditate on just that one word until it sticks; For me that one word was "***peace***", allowing the word to penetrate to the core of you and when we do that, the word will keep us. Maybe you've lost someone close to you, maybe you have a child, he/she is facing 20yrs in prison. Jesus! Maybe you lost your job and your house been in foreclosure for a year, *JESUS, DESPERATE TIMES*! The doctor says its stage 4 cancer, oh my God! What do you do if someone knocked on your door and your child was harmed and they're in the hospital fighting for their life, Jesus, *DESPERATE TIMES*! What about the one who wants to change but my God, the drugs, the women, the alcohol, that lifestyle, the call of those things, the calls to another person even though you're married, *THIS KIND, THE CALL FROM THESE THINGS IT SEEMS LIKE*

YOU JUST CAN'T SHAKE. My God, *DESPERATE!* I can recall a desperate time and all I could do was call on God. I laid on the floor for days, I couldn't sleep, and I wouldn't eat, only crying to the Lord, calling out to Him. You got to fall on your knees and give it to God, and what He tells you to do, do it. It will be the right way, the best for the situation, as God is all knowing and all truth, desperate times, calls for a desperate prayer!

Prayer:

Father, Father, Father. Sometimes we don't know what words to say or what to do Lord. Sometimes I just wanna sit in Your presence and let You comfort me, let Your Holy Spirit minister to me and instruct me, because I don't have the answers and if I knew I could get my own self out of these sticky situations, I would, but I don't, so I'm calling on You. The only consistent help I know. I know that You know all about it, I'm confident about that. That You know all and see all. God sometimes it seems like this life and these situations have overtaken us. Come God, wrap Your arms around me Jesus. Hold me God, God please don't leave, please don't let go, I won't make it if You let go of me. Save me from myself, save me from what is trying to succumb me, save me from the plans of the enemy and deliver me. Not only deliver me but uplift me. When You do it Father, I'll give You the glory, let this be a testimony that will help deliver others. And like Your son Jesus prayed, not my will, but Thy will, let Your will be done. Take what's broken and fix it, and when You do it, I know it will be done right. Heal and set free, change my ways and my situations, give us the victory in this situation, God even if You must do it for Your name's sake God. Thank You, Father, that the word says You do all things well, so we place our life in Your hands, we place these situations that seem so impossible at the altar and say have Your way. In Jesus Name we pray. We worship You even now for what You're going to do, Amen.

My personal confession(s):

My next steps:

Self-Help Prayer

The enemy will have you so down sometimes that all you can focus on is what you haven't done, what's not right and the mistakes. But the devil is a lair, the word says he comes to kill, steal, and destroy. He will try to kill dreams, goals, and have you so stressed out that all you can do is sit and cry. He will try to steal your peace and joy or destroy how you feel about yourself and loved ones. Sometimes you must get to a point where you say, "devil, enough is enough", and everything he says to you, you denounce it. Or whatever negative feeling you feel about you, denounce it. Maybe you don't have the support that you would like, maybe you don't have all the confidence as others and maybe you don't have all the resources. But you can get started. Get up, anoint your head, pray, and help yourself. You may feel you are without help but God is always your greatest help, always have been and always will be. A present help in the time of trouble, Psalms 46:1.

Lean and depend on God for the help. Pray to Him about it. I will look to the hills from whence cometh my help, my help cometh from the Lord who made heaven and earth, Psalms 121.

Prayer:

Lord help me. I need You, I can't do this by myself, I need Your help to guide me, strengthen me, to teach me, to be my help and be my provider, help me to stand. Carry me Lord when I'm weak and help me to be strong. Your word says I can do all things through Christ which strengthens me, Philippians 4:13. Help me to get through the things I need to get through. Give me the confidence I need to build myself up where I may have been torn down. When I feel like I can't do it, give me a word to encourage myself. If it's my past, send me ways to move into a future in You. If it's my own thinking, help me to think good thoughts about myself, replace my negative thinking of I can't succeed or I can't make it with what You said about me. Surround me with great people who pour positive energy and spiritual food into my life, build me up. Help me to overcome every obstacle that may stand in my way and figure out a solution with Your help Lord. You are my everything, I put all my faith, all my trust in You. My life is in Your hands Lord, take my life and shape it to honor You and bring You glory. God, at times when I feel like I don't have the strength to pray for myself, God minister to me, wrap Your arms around me and don't let go. Hold me up until I can stand on my own, in my own strength. Increase my faith, help me to become the best version of myself. I will make it. I can do it. Order my steps Lord. In Jesus Name, Amen.

My personal confession:

My next step:

Sacrificial Prayer

Sacrifice is defined as the act of giving up something valued for the sake of something else regarded as more important or worthy. Just as we offer God a sacrifice of praise and monetary sacrificial offerings. We should offer a sacrifice of prayer as well. Carve out time for it, if someone ask you to pray for them, I learnt this as I grew in my walk, don't wait because the cares of life may overtake you and you may forget. If possible, take them aside and do it instantly. If not, you can take the time immediately and go to God. Go to a quiet place where you can be alone. I take it very seriously when people ask. Although you don't know what it is they may be asking for regarding prayer, that is irrelevant, you can still go to God on their behalf. Sometimes God will show you and God has certainly shown other people what I was bringing to them, and I didn't tell them.

Now of course, in our praise and prayer life these are not the only ways we sacrifice unto the

Lord. Our resources, time, our very lives, and our bodies. The money and the means to the income God blesses us so that "there is meat in thy house" so that the house of God can be well tended to and so the work God wants to do can be done. Sometimes we will have to sacrifice things like going out with friends to take on time to get before the Lord, time to study because a Christian or Preacher who has not labored in the word consistently, it can make you ineffective. It must be a regular part of your schedule. I make time. Then when it comes to our lives, I'm married to the Lord, it's my sacrifice. There is no amount of sacrifice that can add up to the cost of our grace and mercy. I'm happy and content. Only God knows if marriage is in my future, but it's not a focal point, my focus is Jesus, I have too much work to do for the Lord. I chose to dedicate my life to the things of God. I choose to sacrifice myself because what I believe. Count your bodies a living sacrifice, holy and acceptable unto God which is our reasonable service, Romans 12:1.

Prayer:

God, we come to You freely, we come to You humbly, we come to You dying to ourselves. Freely give our time to the work of the Lord, freely give the resources You have allowed us to attain. God, You have been so good to us, no amount of money or time could add up to the ultimate gift You have given us, the gift of life through Your Son Jesus. Thank You, Father, and just as You counted it not robbery to give Your only Son, I now sacrifice my all for Your glory. As without You I'm nothing. Take our lives and raise us up for the kingdom of God. Be pleased with our sacrifice Lord and with us, In Jesus Name, Amen.

My personal confession(s):

My next steps:

Enemies Prayer

Jesus said forgive them for they know not what they do, Luke 23:24. However, some people do mean evil against others. The works of the flesh (Galatians 5:19) is part to blame. Envy, jealousy, hatred etc. All work through us because we allow it to take over. We can cause our mind to think a certain way. Other reasons this happens is because they choose to be controlled by the devil instead of being led by the Spirit. The word says: You are of your father, the devil (John 8:44) and so when some do evil it let us know they are following their father and not God the Father, Amen. I've struggled with this in the past. And I was able to overcome with help. I would return evil for evil, when someone did something to hurt me, I would return the hurt. But as I grew and matured, as well as a great support system, I changed up my game plan when people bring hurt. I learned to keep my hope and trust, belief in God, even when the enemies and trials and test came, remembering what the word says and what God has said matters the most at times like this and it will keep you if you allow it to work in your life. I said if you allow because your flesh will rise up, but you have to have enough wisdom in you and enough word in you to remind you that you are a child of God and this is how I will handle this, God's way. Allow your spirit to be bigger than what your flesh is telling you to do when you are attacked. I posed some questions some time back that said, *DO YOU KNOW HOW TO QUIET YOUR SPIRIT WHEN YOUR FLESH SAYS SNAP?* Or you want to do right but then you end up going off. When those triggers hit your brain and you're headed to 10, we must have control to bring it down, they're at war and we must let our spirit win the fight. Your battle doesn't begin when you are attacked by your enemies, A soldier that is scheduled for battle goes through boot camp and training to prepare for war and in the same way, we must do so. be ready to battle, I feel this way about prayer too, always be in the right frame of mind as a leader, minister, child of God to lift someone up, if they ask or not. But for the battle, you must stay prayed up, stay full of the word so your preparing starts before you are even faced with the attack. Before your Judas betrays you, be ready. There are three types of Judas: 1. the silent Judas, 2. undercover Judas, and 3. secret Judas. The silent Judas sits and watches quietly harboring hatred, envy, jealousy, ill will against you. The undercover Judas are people who gossip about you behind your back, then come back, grin with you, and talk to you like they did nothing wrong and people who are gossipers in general is of this spirit as well. Last, we have secret enemies, this one hurts the most, it could be a close friend, people you've share your business with, waiting to take what you shared and use it against you, people you associate with, people you hang with. Deep down they feel some type of way about you, and it reveals itself, you just have to pay attention, watch and pray, observe their attitudes or actions against you, their support or lack thereof, it all speaks. Lord help us! The word says you will see the downfall of your enemies, Psalms 37. Don't be ignorant of his devices, this is something we will have to continually deal with. Jesus, He used the word and so we will need to. *IT IS WRITTEN*, Matthew 4. I say this because the word said, and he departed for a *SEASON*, Luke 4:13(KJV). That means he's coming back with more power, more attacks. Are you going to be ready or be defeated?

Let the Judas(s) in your life demolish themselves like Jesus's Judas who went back and tried to give the money back "*AFTER*" he realized what he had done, he went and killed himself, Matthew 27.

Prayer:

God, we bless Your Holy Name, thank You for Your word, which tells us what to do when it comes to our enemies. God, we thank You, that we are victorious only in You. God, we thank You that every person and everything that revolts against us shall be defeated, shall be condemned, every scheme, every disruption, all discord, shall be cast down and shall not work. Every spirit like the evil one that seeks to destroy: shut down. The weapons, the gossip, the rumors that may be said, they may form but they won't prosper. God, I trust and believe You, I believe Your plan is the right way. God Your word doesn't contradict, and Your word says I will bless You in the presence of thy enemies. Help us to see our struggles and our trials, even our enemies in a different way. Give us the strength to pray even for those that mean ill will and harm to us. God, we know it's a plot to get our mind off You, but You want us to pass the test so even when we're tested when dealing with people who hate us without a cause. Help us to continue in love and continue in grace, see that our joy remains, even during times like these. Because the joy comes from You and not people.

I prophecy what the devil means to break you down, to tear you down, what the devil sends to push you back and take you back to your past, whatever the devil uses, won't work. I prophecy if you stay in your peace, if you keep your mind on God you will succeed, you will flourish, you will gain, no lack will come to you or your seed. Pray and as much as lies within you be at peace with all men. Father we thank You that You are a good God that when we pass these tests it's a new level in God, new level of faith, new level of worship, new level to God's glory. So, help us to remember as with Jesus the purpose for the enemies that come our way. We give You thanks even through this, when we've been talked about, when our feelings have been hurt, when people take what we say and switch it up. We still raise our head up high and give You glory and praise. It, along with Your word, will carry us through. Protect & keep us, In Jesus Name. Amen.

My personal confession(s):

My next steps:

Singles Prayer:

Some of us are single & looking, single & content, single again, single with kids, single & dating. No matter the category, I'd like to share about the flesh and the single season. Because I believe whether its overeating, overcoming sexual desires, dealing with emotions of anger, sadness, or maybe depression because you don't have a spouse, physical health, etc. A lot of things in this season surrounds the flesh. It's like if someone tickles your tummy and you're ticklish, you're going to start laughing and move your hands, arms, feet, head, your entire body probably. In the same way is the flesh. It affects not just one area but can affect many. I think for a lot of singles, marriage is a priority. ***We must mature and grow to God being our priority***. (See 1 Corinthians 13:11) There were times in my past, when I didn't *CHOOSE GOD AS THE PRIORITY*, (Have no other gods before me, Exodus 20:3). We put men, women, work, tv shows, and idleness, above God's stuff. Some things trip singles up because many haven't disciplined the flesh. Once you master that, you can run on and see what the Lord has in store for you. When I was found, I was not looking, I was serving. I was a singles ministry leader; I was on fire. I was ushering, teaching teenage Sunday school (which I loved), singing in the choir, feeding the homeless with my own money, visiting nursing homes and making fruit baskets for them, keeping them company, praying, and sharing a word. So, get to work there is so much to do. I also did a lot of traveling, kickboxing classes, my businesses started in my singleness season also. And it's so important to love on yourself, all of you, and heal so Gods plans for your life can manifest. For some singles it won't be marriage, see 1 Corinthians 7:8. When God is ready to give you a spouse, He's going make sure you're in the right place. But in the meantime, there is a long list of things you can do to work on yourself. After all these years and single again. I'm still doing work. Adding points on my credit, setting myself up to be a homeowner, working on my 401k. There is so much to do. I don't entertain certain things that could lead to temptation either. Such as, I chose a certain type of lifestyle, music that leads to temptation, I refrain from. My close circle of friends is not worldly, etc. and I have pet scriptures: I walk, feed, and talk to them. *IM SO SERIOUS*! This season can be a very happy, prosperous, and fulfilling one. I experienced the most blessings and favor in my season of singleness. Let us pray.

Prayer:

God, You are the best husband. Lord help us, You know all about us, You know our desires, You know our strengths, our weaknesses. Some of us want to just walk in oneness with You, some desire a spouse, prepare them and help them to be found in Jesus Name. I ask a special blessing for the single person reading this Lord, go through their minds and erase anything that's not like You that would cause them to stumble. I speak pure and Holy, tried, and true. Blessed and highly favored singles. Cool, save, sassy, Red bottom shoes, shoe fetish save and filled with the Holy Ghost, 22inch weave save and Holy. God, let us be like Job. Have you considered my servant Job? God test us and see. In our finances, just as You've shown me and You have no respect of persons, show them radical blessings, before they ask for it, give it because You already know the plan. Lord, You said I'll open the windows of heaven and pour you out a blessing you won't have room enough to receive, Malachi 3: 10. God let the desires for You, be stronger than any other thing in our life. Speak to us Lord, I say this with conviction because I know Lord if we get just this one piece of the puzzle You will work out the other pieces and the picture will be finished. Help single women to remember that they belong to God first. Our commitment is to God first, *LETS DO THAT RELATIONSHIP RIGHT, FIRST. AMEN?*

He shows us how we are to be loved first through Him, then our fathers, then spouses, be it Gods will. Let single women know they are wonderfully made, designed like fine wine no matter the age, tall or short, plump, or skinny. The best beauty comes out when you are being yourself. Heal our hearts God and remove the ashes like Cinderella, polish and clean us up, not focusing on the outside primarily Lord, but first and foremost the inner beauty, the inner most important work. Help single men to be noble with great character and high standards of integrity. Being an example of the love Christs has for the church and gave Himself for it. Selfless men, men who know how to pray, men feeding their minds with the word, so they know how to choose and how to be good husbands that love God, put Him first, and die to Him daily. Lord, I know You to be a keeper and a healer and I thank You in advance that You will also do the same for the person reading this prayer. Enlighten their minds with witty ideas while they wait, show them the next step, in Jesus' name. Perfect everything concerning them Lord. Thank You for grace and mercy so we can go ahead and live, be what You called us to be. We love and thank You for keeping us in this season. I speak blessings and contentment. I pray that You will anoint them for whatever calling You have placed on their lives, I pray that You affirm and reaffirm the love, that is everlasting and can only be found in You. So, help us to develop that relationship and we will find great joy and fulfillment. In Jesus Name, Amen.

My personal confession(s):

My next steps:

Peace Prayer

The absence of peace in a situation is an indication from the Holy Spirit that something is not right. When your gas needle falls low or close to E, most vehicles give you a warning sign that shows a "lit up gas pump" In the same way we have a permanent warning system, a permanent help in us saying, attention is needed.

Gods' peace, the word tells us, is not like the peace that the world gives, John 14:27. He said I will give you peace that surpasses all understanding, Philippians 4:7. People wonder how you made it through catastrophic situations, how you still have your right mind after what they know you went through. It will have people trying to wrap their brains around why you haven't lost your mind yet. When your spirit is not at ease, no peace is there also. Sometimes it could be that you need more information, or maybe need to ask more questions or it's the wrong timing. It could also be the warning about something. Whatever it may be the result should be the same. Go before God in prayer as to why. There should be a pause in whatever you were not at peace about. The bible mentions also that the Holy Spirit warns, shares truth, guides and directs, we just have to listen and recognize. Sometimes that lack of peace is for our protection, Amen.

Prayer:

God, I pray that you would guide us into all truth. Reveal what needs to be seen in the area of the lack of peace. Protect us and direct us, God give us wisdom and understanding that when You are trying to show us Your plan or Your will, to go left or to go right, whatever it may be, let us be wise enough to know what You are trying to say and quiet our lives so we can know that it's You and hear clearly. We thank You that we have a guide that reveals all truth, and we thank You that when we call: You answer, You will protect us by revelation, by putting up a stop sign and we have to be disciplined to see, hear, and act. God, we thank You for Your love, You love us so much that You set up a plan for our entire life and its perfect, when that plan, whether by our own doing or others detour, You send signs. Help us to read Your signs and nudges. Thank You for Your grace and mercy because sometimes we move ahead in things where there was no peace, and it causes havoc in our lives. So, help us to be patient and content, we move too fast in past things which we never should have moved past. Grow us closer to You and wise in the things of God and Your word. We speak peace in the lives of those reading this book. Peace in their minds, still their minds, quiet their minds, a focused mind, stayed on You and peace will follow. God, we thank You that You will give perfect peace that doesn't waver, that comforts during a storm, when we keep our mind stayed on You. That brings us peace, let us seek counsel and wise men and women of God for clarity and better understanding. In Jesus Name, Amen.

My personal confession(s):

My next steps:

Healing Prayer

I believe God. He delivers on His promises to heal, performing miracles, and deliverance. The promises of God are yea and Amen, 2 Corinthians 1:20. If God be for us, who can be against us, Romans 8:31-39. When we go to check ups and get results and get news from the doctors regarding our health, sometimes we worry, we get concerned. Sometimes there can be things to correct the issue with diet and exercise, sometimes surgery is needed. We need to pray and fast. I had a few scares when they tested me for diabetes, and I went on a fast. The test came back negative, but I remember how I felt just hearing they wanted to test me for it. Also, I had a scare with breast cancer as they called me after my mammogram saying they saw unfavorable results and need more tests. I went back in for more tests and I prayed, I also said "either way, I'm gone praise You" the doctors assistant came back 2 or 3 times saying they need more tests. Thank God all tests came back negative. Choose to stand on Gods promises. Keep your mind filled with His goodness, study what the word says on healing, Jesus's miracles of healing. These are not times to be alone, its times to call on prayer warriors and gather in spirit or physically because that's where the power lies, Matthew 18:20.

Prayer:

God, we thank You for doctors and those we can go to for our health, guide the doctor's hands, bless their hands, give them supernatural vision, to see and hear what needs to be seen, to come up with plans and treatments for those in need. God You are the great physician, and You do all things well. Father intervene on behalf of (insert name), our loved ones, our families. God work through body systems, dry up cancer cells, tumors, diabetes, heart diseases, heart attacks, heart failure, even broken hearts God, high blood pressure, regulate body systems; every blood vessel, every organ, God, heal lung cancer, breast cancer. Heal us for

Your glory. To do Your will God. All manner of diseases, heal Father, release Your power, in every area of our lives heal us. MS, Leukemia, Sickle cell, heal Father. Touch sick babies Lord, touch all the sick. Even asthma, and breathing ailments, heal God. God even healing of the minds, touch Lord, renew minds and regulate them. Give us wisdom, knowledge, and whatever we may be able to do to change the disease/ disorders give us strength to do so. Father You are a good God, and we thank You for Your grace and mercy, we thank You in advance for healing us and our loved ones. We declare we will see our children grow into adults and grand kids, we will have long life and good health, blessed in our bodies, in our minds, our family and church family. Blessed, happy, healed of all manner of disease and we cast it down. Devil we cast you out our bodies, our minds, our home, and churches. God have Your way. We plead the blood of Jesus over our lives, family, church family, friends and anyone connected to us, Amen.

For Self:

I declare, I ___ (INSERT NAME) ____ am healed IN JESUS NAME!

Declare your healing today: God I humbly come to You, I (insert name), shall live and not die, what You've started in me, it shall be completed. I shall see God working this out for me, God is my Healer, and He has never failed, nor will He ever. I shall see God's power working in my life. I will obtain favor and a good report. God, I believe and trust everything You say about me, and every promise shall be manifested. I shall see what I read about, I shall see miracles, I will have a testimony after this, In Jesus Name, Amen.

My personal confession(s):

My next steps:

Salvation Prayer

Many reading this book, may not know the Lord. He desires a relationship with you, and we need Him to help us in life. How will we know right from wrong without God? We need Him to direct us. God wants us to experience a blessed life, not wandering like there was no reason He sent us here. I know the plans I have for you sayeth the Lord, plans for a hope and a future to bring you to an expected end, Jeremiah 29:11. From a sincere heart, ask Him to come into your life, ask for forgiveness of sins and by faith believing that God sent His Son, Jesus, to die for our sins and you will be saved. God has no respect of persons, what He has done for one child of His, He will also do for the next without favoritism. Acts 4:12(KJV) says; Neither is their salvation in any other; for there is none other name under heaven given among men, whereby we must be saved. Romans 3:23-24 says, for all have sinned, and come short of the glory of God, 24. Being justified (just as if you never did it) freely by His Grace through the redemption that is in Christ Jesus.

We offer Jesus Christ to you!

I, ________________, believe you died for my sins, forgive me for my shortcomings, come into my life, I accept you as my redeemer, as my Saviour.

Prayer:

God, I pray for this person who just committed their life to You. God, I pray that You would place them in a church that teaches the Word of God just like You did for me. God, I pray that they walk in their new life, if any man be in Christ he is a new creature, old things are passed away and now all things have become new, 2

Corinthians 5:17. God, bring great blessings into this person's life, meet all of their needs, go beyond what they are thinking like You did for me, keep them safe God, send mighty spirit filled people in their life. Speak to them Lord, show them miracles, signs, and wonders. Be with them day by day Lord and build them up in You. We thank You for their life Lord, In Jesus Name, Amen. (Copy this page & send via email so we can pray for you and send you a free gift)

My personal confession(s)

My next steps:

Chapter 5

Examples in the Bible

Going to God in prayer sometimes we feel like we don't know what we should pray for, the Bible says so. Romans 8:26 (KJV), Likewise, the Spirit also helpeth our infirmities: for we know not what we should pray for as we ought: but the Spirit itself maketh intercession for us with groanings which cannot be uttered. So, we must get into the presence of God. I've felt the Holy Spirit in prayer, in studying, during worship at home, the car, and of course at church as well as during fasting. Ask Him to give you the words to say also. I went to work one day, me and a coworker had conversations between clients. She knew I was a Christian, but she didn't know I was writing a book. As I listened, one of the things she said was, "I don't know how to pray". Then the walls came down, she went into details of being mad with God because He hadn't given her and her spouse a child, but He blessed a family member who wasn't married. God led me to share a testimony with her after many things she shared with me. If you listen to people closely you can hear their cries, you can know how to help. I ministered to her about my experience with infertility and this chapter is dedicated to her. I finally told her about my book, I waited to share that because I wanted her to know what God had done more than the book. I'm not the star, God is. The limelight doesn't shine on us, we must make sure it centerstage's God.

Revelation 12:11 (KJV), and they overcame him by the blood of the Lamb and by the words of their testimony and loved not their lives unto the death.

This book is specifically for people like her. Who want to pray but don't know what to say, where to begin. Some start prayer with a topic when I was on the prayer team at my church. I would get up an hour earlier than when I was supposed to so I could study and pray to know what to say and what word to share. Sometimes starting the night before. Some do word searches like fasting, but not quite ready for just water for 7 days, then Daniel fast with veggies may be suitable. Maybe something in your community like the killing of African American men. I found myself praying a lot more for my sons, or maybe political events; praying for the President or schools, with covid and kids going back, or life situations where a loved one is going through, sometimes they will ask for prayer and sometimes not, but intercessors already know we need to pray for them, Amen. So, all these can lead you in your prayer time. Then, the examples that we have been given that we can look back and see how those in the Bible prayed. Let's jump right in.

Solomon's Prayer

1Kings 3: 6. And Solomon said, thou hast shewed unto thy servant David my father great mercy, according as he walked before thee in truth, and in righteousness, and in uprightness of heart with thee; and thou hast kept for him this great kindness, that thou hast given him a son to sit on his throne, as *it is* this day. **7.** And now, O LORD my God, thou hast made thy servant king instead of David my father: and I *am but* a little child: I know not *how* to go out or come in. **8.** And thy servant *is* in the midst of thy people which thou hast chosen, a great people, that cannot be numbered nor counted for multitude. **9.** Give therefore thy servant an understanding heart to judge thy people, that I may discern between good and bad: for who is able to judge this thy so great a people? **10.** And the speech pleased the Lord, that Solomon had asked this thing. **11.** And God said unto him, Because thou hast asked this thing, and hast not asked for thyself long life; neither hast asked riches for thyself, nor hast asked the life of thine enemies; but hast asked for thyself understanding to discern judgment; **12.** Behold, I have done according to thy words: lo, I have given thee a wise and an understanding heart; so that there was none like thee before thee, neither after thee shall any arise like unto thee. **13.** And I have also given thee that which thou hast not asked, both riches, and honour: so that there shall not be any among the kings like unto thee all thy days. **14.** And if thou wilt walk in my ways, to keep my statutes and my commandments, as thy father David did walk, then I will lengthen thy days.

How would you handle an anointing on your child?

How Solomon prayed:

- Talked to God about what He did in the past
- Explained to God some frustrations
- Prayed for understanding and discernment
- Because "what" he prayed for pleased the Lord, God answered his prayer.

Jacob's Prayer

Genesis 32: 9. And Jacob said, O God of my father Abraham, and God of my father Isaac, the LORD which saidst unto me, return unto thy country, and to thy kindred, and I will deal well with thee: **10.** I am not worthy of the least of all the mercies, and of all the truth, which thou hast shewed unto thy servant; for with my staff, I passed over this Jordan; and now I am become two bands. **11.** Deliver me, I pray thee, from the hand of my brother, from the hand of Esau: for I fear him, lest he come and smite me, *and* the mother with the children. **12**. And thou saidst, I will surely do thee good, and make thy seed as the sand of the sea, which cannot be numbered for multitude. **22.** And he rose that night, and took his two wives, and his two women servants, and his eleven sons, and passed over the ford Jabbok. **23.** And he took them, and sent them over the brook, and sent over that he had. **24.** And Jacob was left alone; and there wrestled a man with him until the breaking of the day. **25.** And when he saw that he prevailed not against him, he touched the hollow of his thigh; and the hollow of Jacob's thigh was out of joint, as he wrestled with him. **26.** And he said, let me go, for the day breaketh. And he said, I will not let thee go, except thou bless me. **27.** And he said unto him, what *is* thy name? And he said, Jacob. **28.** And he said, thy name shall be called no more Jacob, but Israel: for as a prince hast thou power with God and with men, and hast prevailed. **29.** And Jacob asked *him*, and said, tell *me*, I pray thee, thy name. And he said, wherefore *is* it *that* thou dost ask after my name? And he blessed him there.

What may have happened if Jacob didn't follow what God said?

How Jacob prayed:

- Spoke back to God what He said to him
- Prayed with humility
- Prayed for deliverance
- Prayed for a blessing

David's Prayer

Psalms 31: 1. In thee, O LORD, do I put my trust; let me never be ashamed: deliver me in thy righteousness. **2.** Bow down thine ear to me; deliver me speedily: be thou my strong rock, for a house of defence to save me. **3.** For thou *art* my rock and my fortress; therefore, for thy name's sake lead me, and guide me. **4.** Pull me out of the net that they have laid privily for me: for thou *art* my strength. **5.** Into thine hand I commit my spirit: thou hast redeemed me, O LORD God of truth. **6.** I have hated them that regard lying vanities: but I trust in the LORD. **7.** I will be glad and rejoice in thy mercy: for thou hast considered my trouble; thou hast known my soul in adversities; **8.** And hast not shut me up into the hand of the enemy: thou hast set my feet in a large room. **9.** Have mercy upon me, O LORD, for I am in trouble: mine eye is consumed with grief, *yea*, my soul, and my belly. **10.** For my life is spent with grief, and my years with sighing: my strength faileth because of mine iniquity, and my bones are consumed. **11.** I was a reproach among all mine enemies, but especially among my neighbours, and a fear to mine acquaintance: they that did see me without fled from me. **12.** I am forgotten as a dead man out of mind: I am like a broken vessel. **13.** For I have heard the slander of many: fear *was* on every side: while they took counsel together against me, they devised to take away my life. **14.** But I trusted in thee, O LORD: I said, Thou *art* my God. **15.** My times *are* in thy hand: deliver me from the hand of mine enemies, and from them that persecute me.

16. Make thy face to shine upon thy servant: save me for thy mercies' sake. **17.** Let me not be ashamed, O LORD; for I have called upon thee: let the wicked be ashamed and let them be silent in the grave._**18.** Let the lying lips be put to silence, which speak grievous things proudly and contemptuously against the righteous! **20.** Thou shalt hide them in the secret of thy presence from the pride of man: thou shalt keep them secretly in a pavilion from the strife of tongues. **21.** Blessed *be* the LORD: for he hath shewed me his marvellous kindness in a strong city. **22.** For I said in my haste, I am cut off from before thine eyes: nevertheless, thou heardest the voice of my supplications when I cried unto thee. **23.** O love the LORD, all ye his saints: *for* the LORD preserveth the faithful, and plentifully rewardeth the proud doer.

Why was David considered, a man after Gods own heart?

How David prayed:

- Very specific in his prayers
- Prayed "search me, Lord", Psalms 139
- Prayed for deliverance
- Reaffirmed his belief

Daniel's Prayer

Daniel 9: **3.** And I set my face unto the Lord God, to seek by prayer and supplications, with fasting, and sackcloth, and ashes: **4.** And I prayed unto the LORD my God, and made my confession, and said, O Lord, the great and dreadful God, keeping the covenant and mercy to them that love him, and to them that keep his commandments; **5.** We have sinned, and have committed iniquity, and have done wickedly, and have rebelled, even by departing from thy precepts and from thy judgments: **6.** Neither have we hearkened unto thy servants the prophets, which spake in thy name to our kings, our princes, and our fathers, and to all the people of the land.

7. O Lord, righteousness *belongeth* unto thee, but unto us confusion of faces, as at this day; to the men of Judah, and to the inhabitants of Jerusalem, and unto all Israel, *that are* near, and *that are* far off, through all the countries wither thou has driven them, because of their trespass that they have trespassed against thee. **8.** O Lord, to us *belongeth* confusion of face, to our kings, to our princes, and to our fathers, because we have sinned against thee. **9.** To the Lord our God *belong* mercies and forgivenesses, though we

have rebelled against him; **13.** As *it is* written in the law of Moses, all this evil is come upon us: yet made we not our prayer before the LORD our God, that we might turn from our iniquities, and understand thy truth. **14.** Therefore, hath the LORD watched upon the evil, and brought it upon us: for the LORD our God *is* righteous in all his works which he doeth: for we obeyed not his voice. **15.** And now, O Lord our God, that hast brought thy people forth out of the land of Egypt with a mighty hand, and hast gotten thee renown, as at this day; we have sinned, we have done wickedly. **16.** O Lord, according to all thy righteousness, I beseech thee, let thine anger and thy fury be turned away from thy city Jerusalem, thy holy mountain: because for our sins, and for the iniquities of our fathers, Jerusalem and thy people *are become* a reproach to all *that are* about us. **17.** Now therefore, O our God, hear the prayer of thy servant, and his supplications, and cause thy face to shine upon thy sanctuary that is desolate, for the Lord's sake. **18.**

O my God, incline thine ear, and hear; open thine eyes, and behold our desolations, and the city which is called by thy name: for we do not present our supplications before thee for our righteousnesses, but for thy great mercies. **19.** O Lord, hear; O Lord, forgive; O Lord, hearken and do; defer not, for thine own sake

Had Daniel not prayed, what may have been the outcome?

How Daniel prayed:

- He exalted God
- He confessed his sins to the Lord
- He even confessed the sins of others on their behalf unto the Lord
- He asked the Lord for forgiveness
- He repented before the Lord
- He cried out to the Lord for mercy and to hear his pray
- He prayed unto God to turn his anger away from them

- He prayed on behalf of others
- He prayed that God would answer for His Name's sake

Hannah's Prayer

1Samuel 1: 10. And she *was* in bitterness of soul, and prayed unto the LORD, and wept sore. **11.** And she vowed a vow, and said, O LORD of hosts, if thou wilt indeed look on the affliction of thine handmaid, and remember me, and not forget thine handmaid, but wilt give unto thine handmaid a man child, then I will give him unto the LORD all the days of his life, and there shall no razor come upon his head.**12.** And it came to pass, as she continued praying before the LORD, that Eli marked her mouth. **13.** Now Hannah, she spake in her heart; only her lips moved, but her voice was not heard therefore, Eli thought she had been drunken. **14.** And Eli said unto her, how long wilt thou be drunken? put away thy wine from thee. **15.** And Hannah answered and said, no, my lord, I *am* a woman of a sorrowful spirit: I have drunk neither wine nor strong drink but have poured out my soul before the LORD. **16.** Count not thine handmaid for a daughter of Belial: for out of the abundance of my complaint and grief have I spoken hitherto. **17.** Then Eli answered and said, go in peace: and the God of Israel grant *thee* thy petition that thou hast asked of him**19.** And they rose in the morning early, and worshipped before the LORD, and returned, and came to their house to Ramah: and Elkanah knew Hannah his wife; and the LORD remembered her. **20.** Wherefore it came to pass, when the time was come about after Hannah had conceived, that she bare a son, and called his name Samuel, *saying*, Because I have asked him of the LORD. **21.** And the man Elkanah, and all his house, went up to offer unto the LORD the yearly sacrifice, and his vow. **22.** But Hannah went not up; for she said unto her husband, *I will not go up* until the child be weaned, and *then* I will bring him, that he may appear before the LORD, and there abide forever **26.** And she said, oh my lord, *as* thy soul liveth, my lord, I *am* the woman that stood by thee here, praying unto the LORD. **27.** For this child I prayed; and the LORD hath given me my petition which I asked of him: **28.** Therefore, also I have lent him to the LORD if he liveth he shall be lent to the LORD. And he worshipped the LORD there.

What vow(s) have you made unto the Lord?

How Hannah prayed:

- Cried out to the Lord and asked the Lord to remember her
- Made a vow unto the Lord
- She petitioned God about her desires; Others took her petition to the Lord
- She asked the Lord to look on her pain, suffering and her ailment.

Jesus Prayer

Matthew 27: 46. And about the ninth hour Jesus cried with a loud voice, saying, Eli, Eli, lama sabachthani? That is to say, My God, my God, why hast thou forsaken me. **50.** Jesus, when he had cried again with a loud voice, yielded up the ghost.

Luke 23: 34. Then Jesus said, "Father, forgive them, for they do not know what they do". And they divided His garments and cast lots.

Matthew 6: 5. And when thou prayest, thou shalt not be as the hypocrites *are* for, they love to pray standing in the synagogues and in the corners of the streets, that they may be seen of men. Verily I say unto you, they have their reward. **6.** But thou, when thou prayest, enter thy closet, and when thou hast shut thy door, pray to thy Father which is in secret; and thy Father which seeth in secret shall reward thee openly. **7.** But when ye pray, use not vain repetitions, as the heathen *do*: for they think that they shall be heard for their much speaking. **8.** Be not ye therefore like unto them: for your Father knoweth what things ye have need of, before ye ask him. **9.** After this manner therefore pray ye: Our Father which art in heaven, Hallowed be thy name.

10. Thy kingdom come. Thy will be done in earth,
as *it is* in heaven. **11.** Give us this day our daily
bread. **12.** And forgive us our debts, as we forgive
our debtors. **13.** And lead us not into temptation
but deliver us from evil: For thine is the kingdom,
and the power, and the glory, forever. Amen.

Do you have a plan on how to share Jesus with others?

How Jesus Prayed:

- Reverenced God
- He prayed for his accused even on His last breaths.
- He asked God questions
- Cried out to God
- Prayed Gods will be done
- Prayed for daily provision
- Prayed for forgiveness
- Prayed for deliverance

Notes:

Questions & Answers

1. I've had some setbacks, does God hear even me?

God tells us in His Word that the prayer of the righteous avails much.

God sees and hears us. In Psalms 34:15 the word says the eyes of the Lord are on the righteous and His ears are attentive to their cry.

2. Why does God not respond to my prayers?

God is not like us; He doesn't think or act the way we do. He loves different and keeps all His promises. He may respond but not in the way we may want Him to. He is not mad at you. He acts according to the plan and will for your life.

-Promises of God are yeah and amen, 2 Corinthians 1:20.

-His anger last only for a moment, Psalms 30:5.

See also Numbers 23:19

3. ***Why do I feel so alone?***

Normally these feelings, which is an emotion, can change. Some come from the devil. We must choose to believe and stand on His promises. The devil can use us to think bad things about our life, ourselves, and others. If we change the way we think, it can change our lives. God has already promised: I will never leave you or forsake you, Hebrews 13:5.

We already have the power to cast down everything the devil sends our way. Whatever things are true, honest, just, pure, lovely, of good report, if there be any virtue, if there be any praise, ***THINK ON THESE THINGS***, Philippians 4:8.

You're never alone. God promises to be with us ***ALWAYS***.

See also Matthew 28: 20. Seeking counsel from your Pastor to help, if you don't have one ask a friend or family you trust for a referral, a Licensed Therapist would help also.

4. *I messed up; how can I get back on track?*

Welcome to the messed-up club. Unfortunately, we all have messed up, we all have been frustrated, mad, said things we shouldn't say, angry, we all have sinned and done things we're not proud of. But thanks, be unto God that you can get right back up and be restored and renewed. The word promises us that He gives Beauty for ashes, Isaiah 61:3. He takes the ugly things that you beat yourself up about and those secret things you don't want to share and turns it into things that will work for your good. Repentance is key. See Romans 10:9, 3:23. Our reconnection is repenting daily, turning from sin, and praying continually.

5. *DOES GOD STILL LOVE ME?*

Absolutely! Romans 8:35-39, Who shall separate us from the Love of Christ? For I am persuaded, that neither death, nor life, nor angels, nor principalities, nor powers, nor things present, nor things to come, nor height, nor depth, nor any other creature, ***SHALL BE ABLE TO SEPARATE US FROM THE LOVE OF GOD, WHICH IS IN CHRIST JESUS OUR LORD.*** "*Nothing*" you do can stop God from loving you. His love is never ending, however, there are consequences to choices we make and things we do.

Resources

National Suicide Prevention Hotline: 800-273-8255

Need counseling or looking for a church home? Email us for resources

For prayer, book tour schedule, book signing events or want a book signing at your church, speaking engagements contact us below, feel free to join our email list for all upcoming events.

Email us: reachinggodthroughprayer@gmail.com
Follow us: YouTube - Michelle Brown Ministries

About the Author

Michelle Brown

Licensed Minister of the Gospel, Mother, and Business Owner. Business Consultant for Salon Management Systems & School Curriculums & Development. Owner of Great Extension Inc., serving all the U.S. Licensed Instructor for the State of NC, Featured in over 30 National trade magazines & publications. Author of 3 industry trade eBooks. National Educator and have taught hundreds of classes throughout the U.S. I Resides in Raleigh, North Carolina.

Made in the USA
Columbia, SC
23 September 2024